Absent
from the
Body

Absent
from the
Body

One Man's Clinical Death,
A Journey Through Heaven and Hell

DON BRUBAKER

Peninsula Publishing / Palmetto, Florida

Additional copies of this book may be ordered through bookstores or by sending $12.95 plus $3.50 shipping and handling to:

Publishers Distribution Service
6893 Sullivan Road
Grawn, MI 49637

Publisher's Cataloging - in - Publication Data
Brubaker, Don
     Absent from the body: one man's clinical death, a journey through heaven and hell
         p.   cm.
       Includes bibliographical references and index.
       ISBN 0-9645438-0-X
       1. Brubaker, Don, 1928-1982. 2. Near-death experiences. 3. Hell. I. Title.
     BF1045.N4B78   1996
     236.25' 092—dc20
     95-68236

Book design and production by
PUBLISHERS DESIGN SERVICE

10 9 8 7 6 5 4 3 2 1

Printed in the United States of America

*This book is dedicated to
our Lord and Savior
Jesus Christ.
We give him
all the praise and all the Glory.*

Contents

❖ CONTENTS ❖

Foreword

OCCASIONALLY the public's attention is riveted by the testimony of someone who has suffered "clinical death" and claims to have gone to heaven. But seldom has anyone come forth after a clinical death experience and recounted a journey into the bowels of hell.

Don Brubaker went to hell and lived to tell about it.

A salesman obsessed with self and success, Don wandered ignorantly into the web of the occult, believing that he was on the road to self-awareness. In the midst of his compulsive pursuit, he was snatched out of this world by a massive heart attack and taken to a place from which no one has ever brought a firsthand account.

"If I ascend up into heaven, thou art there," the Psalmist sang to the Lord. "If I make my bed in hell, behold, thou art there."

Don Brubaker discovered that truth more vividly than anyone in modern history.

Don's body survived his incredible journey, largely unchanged. But Don's spirit was revolutionized by the love of Jesus Christ—a love that reached down into the pit of hell itself to rescue him. In the years that followed, Don gave himself wholly to ministry, to a life of faithful telling and re-telling of the unfathomable love of Christ. Veteran Christians who knew him and worked with him were convinced of his absolute integrity and were often humbled by his thorough dedication to His Master.

One day Don Brubaker telephoned me. "I have a rather unusual story," he began.

That little statement proved to be a whopping understatement.

After listening to Don tell his story, and after combing through his voluminous personal notes, I too was convinced–and humbled.

This is that often incredible story: not a fantasy, although it reads like one, but an account of the facts in a case like no other. In the following pages, you will accompany an ordinary modern man on a most extraordinary journey. Don Brubaker came back a different person. When you come back, you may find that you too have somehow changed.

Wilfred M. Laudrus

WILFRED M. LAUDRUS,
PROFESSOR EMERITUS,
CHAPMAN UNIVERSITY, ORANGE, CALIFORNIA

Acknowledgements

THANK YOU to our nameless benefactor (his request), for without his financial blessings none of this would have been possible. Thanks to my three Angels: Terrie, Cindy & Jeff, who I love with all my heart. Thanks for holding the family together.

Thanks to Bob and Bev for putting up with me all those months. Thank you Tad and Brad King for steering me to Publishers Design Service (P.D.S.). God Bless You. What a great group of people. Mark, Alex and everyone there.

Thanks to the many Prayer Warriors, you know who you are.

And most of all thanks to my Dennie, whose love and support have gone beyond the realm of supernatural understanding.

And, lest we forget all of the doctors and nurses who gave their all, Thank you. And to Dr. Bennett, you never gave up. Thank God you never gave up.

MARY (BRUBAKER) PENNEY

Hugh Downs and the author at radio station
WIAA in Interlochen, Michigan.

Absent
from the
Body

1.

The Good Life

THURSDAY. January 6, 1977. Six in the morning. The alarm clock shakes Don Brubaker from sleep. It's a cold, snow-swept northern Michigan winter day. The warmth of the bed isn't easy to give up. But Don's motivational drive takes over. He has sales calls to make today. A profitable new account is awaiting his attention in Grand Rapids. First, he's got to tie up some loose ends in the office. Don throws off the blankets and rumbles out of bed, toward the shower. His day is dawning.

The view from the picture window of his new home is a breathtaking winter wonderland. The fresh snow delicately laces the trees surrounding the house, nestled out of sight in the small woods. Don still can't help but pause just for a moment between bedroom and kitchen to take in the view. A delicious phrase runs silently through his mind.

"Mine . . . at last."

Things have been rough around here, especially before the last month or two. Don rarely thinks about it now, now that things seem to be achieving picture-perfection. But in the middle of it all, the legal and financial tug-of-war was horrible. Of course, it might not be completely over yet–there is still a lawsuit or two pending. But things have settled down considerably. The worst is over. By sheer determination, founded on rock-solid self-assurance, Don has the sweet satisfaction of knowing he has personally met every challenge. In the stillness of the snowy dawn, he knows he has won.

And then he turns away, to get on with it. His internal engine is already running strong.

The driveway, of course, must be cleared, just as it must after each of these classic Michigan snowstorms. Like a true native of the region, Don declines from grumbling. Instead, he thinks of this too, as a challenge –but a simple and fun one. He mounts his new snow-blower, fires it up like a teen-age hot-rodder, and charges into the snow with youthful glee.

Instinct takes over. Don has done this job so many times that he no longer thinks about it, and the powerful snow machine practically knows the path to take. Don's mind races far, far ahead, into the dream-world of a successful future. This beautiful, secluded home will become his palace. The driveway will need black-topping. Then he will need to put light and heat in the garage, and perhaps the wood shop as well. And there is plenty more to do. Don and his junior high schooler

18

son Jeff have already acquired some beautiful oak. It's drying out in the big walk-out basement.

The snowblower growls on, chewing through the three-foot wall of snow. At such depth, the plowing takes a good while. But time passes quickly for Don Brubaker. He hardly notices the icy air against his boyish 48-year-old face. His work warms him. He thinks it will be a long winter. But it's going to be a good day.

He pulls the tractor back into its resting place as he runs a mental review of the past couple of days of business. He was on the road, visiting clients in the north, since Tuesday morning. Catch-up work from Christmas. Things went reasonably well. He came home with a fistful of new advertising accounts for the television station. He is ahead of the other salesmen for the month. Success agrees with Don.

In many respects, the television station is his own creation. There was the day when Don Brubaker was the only guy selling, the only one willing to take on Traverse City's newest station, a station still struggling to get going. He hustled business after business after business, for hundreds of miles around, deploying the finest, most aggressive sales techniques—to sell commercials on a station that barely existed. His skill and diligence, and really little else, put them on the video map. Today, it is thriving. As is Don.

He stands in the front hallway of the house, sloughing off his bulky work coat in favor of the well-fitted overcoat he wears to the office. There's a mirror by the door, appropriately enough, and Don catches his reflection. He suppresses a chuckle. His eye is still black. He was replacing a light socket in the ceiling last evening, and the whole thing slipped out of his hand. It caught him square on the eye and gave him a heck of a shiner. Anyone else might find it awkward to explain a black eye. But Don is an expert salesman. He will use even this as a conversational ice-breaker.

Don has learned well. He has absorbed the teachings of dozens of motivational books. He and Mary have attended more positive thinking seminars than either of them can count. They know all the speakers on the circuit, some personally. So Don knows well enough that adversity–from a simple black eye to a tangled legal spider web–can be turned into a benefit.

The day is a promising one. Don resolves it to be.

Before turning the doorknob to make his exit, he pauses. He hasn't heard Jeff stirring about getting ready for school. Don turns and steps lightly to Jeff's room. He doesn't want to wake Mary. He will call her later from the station to say good morning, just as he does every day.

He rouses his son from slumber, whispers, "Have a good day, Jeff," and then heads away. This weekend he will enjoy cross-country skiing with the family. But right now, he's got to get going. It's sales time for Traverse City's number one seller of commercial time. Even as he pulls out of the freshly plowed driveway, Don's eyes twinkle a bit. Every morning, as he heads out on another day, he feels that exhilarating whoosh of heady success.

<u>Look out, world!</u>

Tooling down the rural roads toward town, Don's internal engine whirs along in overdrive. He is sailing. He is finally becoming the dynamo he has always wanted to be.

Then, a <u>ping</u> in the engine inside of him. Without warning, an oddness wedges its way into Don's upbeat mindset. It is a low, strange sensation, a whiff of anxiety, like the smell of burning rubber, but one that will not float away. It stays.

Don keeps driving, trying to dismiss the weird feeling as nothing. He pushes the accelerator, still intent on squeezing the most out of his morning. He is never willing to laze along. He wants to get there. Today, the odd gnawing in his mind makes him want to get there even faster.

The anxiety is unexplainable. But it has edged into his consciousness, and it is growing.

He pulls into the company parking lot, sighing slightly with relief, yet unwilling to acknowledge to himself that anything is wrong. Nothing is wrong, after all. He must have eaten something that isn't agreeing with his system.

Inside the secretary has coffee going.

"Morning, Don."

"Good morning!" His usual enthusiastic sales sound.

He picks up his mug, which has been standing ready since he left it at its usual post Monday evening at the end of the workday. Don pours a cup of the brew—black, laced with sugar, as always—and steps to his desk. The uneasiness is creeping along inside of him. He works harder to ignore it.

Even after his marathon snow-plowing effort and his drive in from the outer edges of town, Don Brubaker is the first of the sales crew in the office today. Already, by his private calculations, this is the twenty-third snow-day of the winter that he has been first. The others would regard this as a stupid game, but to the salesman it is an important motivational prod. It feeds the ego. Don's is well fed.

Maybe the damn cigarettes are giving him this crazy feeling, Don figures. Mary nudged him about his habit only days before, during the New Year's holiday.

Don knew even as she spoke that her concern was genuine. She is a good and devoted wife. He knows her well enough to know she isn't nagging. For such a tiny, petite lady, she has always been a tower of strength to him—even during ebb tide.

They have both tried to quit, too. Not recently, but once or twice they have given it a shot. But the pressure is always on in Television Land. Don needs an escape valve. A cigarette is so simple . . .

They also discussed, as he recalls now, his extensive traveling schedule. Don agreed in principle to work with her at improving their lifestyle. He would try to cut down on the alcohol too. Mary has already quit altogether. He would stay home more if he could. And yes, now that he thinks through that whole conversation, he promised to quit smoking.

And yet, the desire to quit isn't even there. Don sits

at his desk, wondering if cigarettes have given him this awful heartburn—and still his visceral response is to long for a cigarette.

He lights his sixth one of the morning. His stomach is swimming in choppy waters. And it is only 9:00 a.m.

Don stands up and steps toward the coffee machine. He tastes a burning at the back of his throat. He loads the coffee with cream, hoping it will help. It doesn't.

The motivational impulse, well-conditioned after all these years, snaps into action.

<u>If I don't settle down,</u> Don warns himself silently, <u>I won't get anything done today!</u>

He picks up the phone and begins dialing sales contacts. He needs work. His system needs to be distracted. A success or two, Don tells himself, will settle this turbulence in the pit of his stomach.

Don checks in with his sales manager to talk over an upcoming presentation to a potential client. They are both clever people, and inevitably they begin trading quips. For a while, Don gets caught up in typical office horseplay. The churning within seems to subside. He breathes easier. Maybe this day will turn out all right after all.

He attacks the mess of papers on his desk with new vigor. One by one he dispenses with them. But with each new page, new sourness spreads throughout his insides. His nerves tingle with irritation. He squeezes his eyes shut, unable to focus on his work. Something is not right at all. <u>What the hell's wrong with me?</u> he growls to himself.

He bolts for the rest room. Maybe he can find relief there. As his feet cross the floor, he feels like he's walking on eggshells. Every nerve ending is alive and aflame.

Don pushes himself into the door labeled MEN. Inside, he is startled by his reflection in the mirror. His face is pasty, ghost-like. The black eye is a stark, glaring purple. Don touches his flesh. It is clammy and gray.

He twists the knob for cold water and splashes it nervously on his face. It feels good and helps some, but it isn't enough. A nausea is crawling over his body. He is gripped by something he has never felt. It is dread.

Fresh air, he tells himself. Maybe some fresh air will help. Without a word he retrieves his coat and hat. Why tell anybody? It's stupid, whatever it is that is giving him such hell. And he knows he will be back in a moment or two.

The brisk Michigan air bites into his face, and his chest cavity begins to burn. He feels the muscles in his chest squeezing him, tighter and tighter. Don blinks, but the cars in the company parking lot are running together in a garish blur.

Suddenly, Don Brubaker knows.

"Heart attack!" he gasps out loud.

The impact of the realization sends his mind reeling. No! Not me! No! No!

The words scream through his head. He is a healthy, 48-year-old man. He doesn't deserve this! Not now. Not Don Brubaker.

His thoughts are desperate.

Maybe if I don't tell anyone, he considers momentarily, anguishing, it'll just go away. It isn't rational, but for a fleeting moment, Don begins to believe it will work. His mind clears, the agitation subsides.

Holding his stomach, as if to keep the tempest still, Don plots his next move. For the moment, his calm, sane self takes over.

Don, you're having a heart attack, a resolute voice seems to say to him. You need to get to the hospital.

He determines not to be an idiot. He will get into his car. He will drive himself to the hospital. He will find out what is really wrong.

As he turns the key and pulls the car into gear, Don realizes the pain has ebbed away. He can see fairly well. He pulls the car out of the lot and begins driving toward the hospital calmly, almost as if nothing is wrong.

The pavement stretches in front of him, and his work ethic begins to nudge him. What if this is a false alarm? He knows how silly he will feel if he has to explain all this to his co-workers. After all, he has a lot of work to do, and an appointment to keep in Grand Rapids. And yet, a sense of urgency is nettling him. He pushes the accelerator pedal closer to the floor.

Don parks, gets out of the car, and walks toward the emergency entrance. The air is freezing, but he feels hot. The closer he gets to the doorway, the slower his legs seem to move. He feels like he is pushing himself through molasses, not quite touching the ground, unable to keep up his speed. But he pushes on. He must hurry. He must flee the pain. It is beginning to pulse again, through his chest, and now down into his left arm.

Hurry . . .

Finally, he is inside. The nurse behind the registration counter looks up blankly.

Don's expression is flat. "I'm having a heart attack," he says in a low monotone.

"Yes sir," she responds, pushing away from her desk and hurrying around the corner toward him. "I believe you are."

The quiet of the hospital is torn away in a matter of moments. Suddenly, he is engulfed by rapid talk and the rustle of nurses' crisp uniforms and the clatter of equipment. Fingers poke him and hurt him. The tiny fishbowl of a room is swirling and frothing with sound and light, brighter and brighter light. A string of staccato questions fire at him through the chaos.

Who are you?

Don struggles to answer. "Don Brubaker."

Who do we contact?

"Mary Brubaker."

Who is your doctor?

"Dr. Douglas."

Where do you work?

Don can't answer. He can't remember. He can't form the words. He expects to hear another question, but someone is turning the volume down. Sounds are fading away. His ear strains to pick out a question. Instead, the activity around him is increasing in pace.

He feels the rubber gripping his arm–blood pressure. Cold metal discs on his chest, his temples–electrocardiogram. A monitor begins to beep. Needles in his arm –intravenous. Don can't keep up with it all. He is swimming in his own limbo.

Dr. Douglas looms above him, smiling.

"Don, this is Dr. Benjamin." Don sees the other doctor now, too. "He's the best in the city. Now just relax, Don, take deep breaths."

Don gulps for air.

"Breathe more slowly," Douglas urges him, his eyes darting all around the fishbowl, searching the heart monitor, the gauges, the needles.

Don corrals his lungs and works hard to breathe in slowly, breathe out slowly, breathe in slowly, breathe out–<u>what a kind man Dr. Douglas is</u>, he says to himself–breathe in slowly, breathe out slowly . . .

Then all the colors run together in front of Don's eyes. The doctor's face droops into his white coat, the pale walls consume the shiny equipment, the fishbowl melts into a blob.

And everything disappears.

* * *

Something cold touches Don's hand, He opens his eyes. Mary is there, holding his hand.

"How long have I been out?" Don asks.

Mary smiles. "Not too long," she responds. "Just relax honey, everything's going to be fine."

Bob, an old friend of the family, is standing next to her, smiling a grim smile.

"Hang in there, Father," Bob says. Bob always calls him Father.

"Don't worry," Mary says, almost insisting. "I'll be right here with you."

Don looks into her small, pretty face. She really doesn't look worried, he notes. Maybe she's right. Maybe he will be okay.

His tongue feels thick. He talks in slow motion.

"I think I feel better," he says, forcing the words to form, "now that you're both here with me." But the sentence tires him, and he can only follow it with a weak grin at the very corners of his mouth.

The ceiling and walls begin to slip away. Someone is moving his bed. Mary and Bob are walking alongside, their faces jostling about in Don's field of vision. He can see Mary's eyebrows begin to knit together, her lips tightening with tension.

The rubber wheels of the gurney sing a solemn note as they roll over the tile of the hallway. A strange sense of peacefulness floats down over him, like a soft linen bed sheet draping itself gently over a bed. He feels safe. He feels good. Something, in fact, might even be tickling him a little, for he wants to giggle. The giddiness is beginning to swarm him, making him light-headed, almost weightless. He is happy to go on this little trip, with Mary walking along beside him and holding his hand.

The ding! of the elevator bell snaps the mood. The elevator doors gape open to accept him and the party scuffing along around him. The elevator closes in around him. Everything is getting dark again. Where is my Mary? <u>Where is Mary?</u> She seems so far away. Don frowns, his eyes prowling the tiny cubicle. All the images are hazy again. He tries to squint through the fog, but he doesn't have the strength. <u>Mary! Where is Mary?</u>

The floor begins to slip away. Don's eyes open wide as he feels the cart picking up speed. He looks over the edge, as the gurney rolls faster and faster downhill. He can see himself lying on the cart—and yet he is still strapped in! The elevator and the medical team are gone—and yet they are still standing around him! Don feels the terror filling his throat, begging to scream. He feels himself being sucked down into a steep tunnel, gurney and all. His body is being pulled down and down and down, and yet pulled back and up. His mind is banging wildly at him for explanations as his senses twist and warp, and his body and soul split apart. There is no time for questioning, no time for answering. Don Brubaker is screaming into an unknown depth, an endless hole, unable to claw his way to a stop. He knows he is alive, but he can not tell how—or why—or where.

Don Brubaker is in hell.

2.

Back in Time

I have been to hell.

My name is Don Brubaker. I am six-feet one-inch tall, one hundred and eighty pounds, with brown hair and blue eyes. I grew up in and around Lincoln, Nebraska, during the years of the dust bowl and the Great Depression. I was raised during a time of extreme austerity. The value of hard work was deeply ingrained in my psyche. My life was also implanted with the seeds of a strong success-oriented drive. The need for material gain, the desperate importance of never allowing my family to go without, were rooted deeply within me.

My older brother and I were enveloped by a close-knit family. My parents were openly loving. We also had a host of affectionate cousins, with all the corresponding aunts and uncles and grandparents. My early years were filled with family reunions in the park, huge holiday celebrations, picnics to beat the band, ice cream socials, and the classic social event of the American midwest—card parties.

What my parents lacked in financial resources, they did their best to make up for in other creative ways.

The country was held in the debilitating grip of economic despair, but it was a fascinating era to grow up in. For my brother Dale and me, there was always something to do, even before the advent of TV. No one was hurried. There were free outdoor movies during the summer, intriguing radio mysteries, secretive discussion of the distant European war. Hobos and gypsy bands wandered through the region. There were newer and faster trains, the excitement and wonder of aeroplanes, and the eye-popping make-believe of Buck Rogers. I was the all-American country boy.

Early in 1940, my family moved to a large farm in southern Iowa. On the farm, there was more work and less play. Chores seemed endless. Modern conveniences –such as indoor plumbing and electricity–had unfortunately been left behind in the city. Still, I was happy. Life was austere, but pleasant enough.

My brother Dale left me behind for World War II. He was headed for the glamorous life of an Air Force pilot. The chores were left to me. Pigs needed slopping, cows wanted milking, the chickens cackled for feed. Fields needed plowing, horses needed rubbing down. Day by day the farm looked smaller.

The itch to get out into the world began to spread in me. The radio and movie news offered a whole new universe of adventure, romance, and success. And I could well imagine that news announcer, with his own personal window on the world, as the most fascinating

32

Don, his brother Dale, and
their cousin Richard.

person on planet earth, living in the very midst of absolutely everything that was happening anywhere—and what a privilege to <u>tell</u> it to the rest of the world!

I wanted a taste of it myself. My best course was obvious. Within the days after graduation from high school, I bent over a recruiter's desk and enlisted in the United States Army. Eight weeks later I was stepping onto Korean soil, my hair cut close to my scalp.

My worldly education had begun.

* * *

The oriental is a fascinating person. To a prairie boy like me, the oriental face itself was mysterious and exotic. But as I trekked from military base to military base in Korea, and later in Japan, I was drawn to the oriental character, its ancient devotion to strange gods. Many of the other soldiers submerged themselves in buddhism and other eastern philosophies. I didn't, but I was interested. I learned a lot. The religion I had known was boring and dull. The mysticism of the East was intriguing, and tempting.

I left the service and headed back to the Iowa farm. With G.I. Bill in hand, I prepared for a virtually free ride to college. I also had a steady girl–a tiny, little miss named Mary. My drive for success was getting off to a good start. I was up and running. Or so I thought.

On a gravel road, in the middle of nowhere, my Oldsmobile spun out of control and began turning somersaults. Doctors were amazed that I had not been crushed to death. My back was badly damaged, and if I lived, they said, I would be paralyzed.

The accident made me mad, and I rejected their prognosis. I had plans. Bigger plans than this! No stupid car wreck was going to stop me.

My girlfriend visited me in the hospital. I could tell she was horrified, but for some reason she believed everything I ever said. I told her I was going to get out of there and marry her. She smiled primly and agreed.

Twelve weeks later I stood at the alter under my own power, with no paralysis, no sign of physical dam-

34

age. I had employed relentlessly positive thinking, and I had climbed out of the hospital bed in record time.

Mary and I were wed on Halloween 1948, a date that might have appealed to some of my mystic friends from the Orient.

Mary would never again leave my side. She was of good midwestern stock, an industrious, sensible girl who had suffered her share of knocks as a kid. She, as much as I, was determined to make this marriage work —and, in fact, soar!

*   *   *

There was little insurance money from the accident. Monstrous hospital expenses seemed to put college well out of reach for the time being. I needed cash. Reluctantly we headed for the farm—the only work I really knew yet—with my pregnant Mary.

My parents, after all, really needed me. They were not the spring chickens they once were. We moved to Colorado with them. But I had dreams of wealth and other thrills that just didn't happen on farms. My loyalties were torn.

And farming, unfulfilling as it was, was not enough. I had to supplement our income by working a long string of ridiculous part-time temporary jobs. I was at various times a carpenter, a surveyor, and one of hundreds of commoners working at a sugar mill. All of which was beneath me—but I could talk my way into just about any job I set sight on.

Mary, always thinking highly of me, prompted me to greater heights. "Why don't you put that talented mouth to work—<u>real</u> work?" she teased one evening.

I looked at her with what must have been a dumb stare. "What do you mean?"

"Why don't you go to work as a radio or television announcer? You've got a penchant for convincing conversation," she said supportively.

I felt odd. That kind of work had been a childhood dream. But I had been working at frivolous, menial jobs and doing farm chores for so long now . . . I wondered if I could really pull it off. Presented with the challenge, I could feel myself instinctively pulling back, lacking confidence.

Mary, however, was sick of farm life. "Look," she finally said firmly, tired of waiting for a decision from me, "it's either me or the cows."

I wound up hunched over a correspondence course at the desk in the spare bedroom, learning broadcasting by mail. I headed for California to the three-month broadcasting school—but I went alone. Mary stayed behind in Colorado with my parents and our two little daughters, Terrie and Cindy.

The long weeks of separation finally ended, and I landed a broadcasting job at a Montana radio station. We packed up once again and headed for Montana, where I could get some practical on-the-job training and experience. There, I picked up a wealth of useful knowledge in the field of communications. Suddenly I found that my diverse background of forgettable jobs would serve me well with my audiences. I could talk just like all the farmers, ranchers, bartenders, trucker, oil-riggers, and teachers in my audience. People liked me. I could tell that I was pretty good.

But in radio, I was a little fish in a big pond. I determined to find a smaller pond.

Johnny, my California instructor and a talented TV personality, had moved to Michigan, and he kindly landed me an interview at a brand-new television station in Traverse City where he was now on the air himself. The interview went beautifully. We Brubakers were moving again.

Don worked as a sports announcer at W.P.B.N.-TV
in Traverse City, MI.1958-61.

We touched down in Traverse City, one of the state's most beautiful resort towns, encircling the "West Arm" of picturesque Grand Traverse Bay. Traverse City had a permanent population of less than twenty thousand, although the tourist trade was active throughout the year and especially thick during the summer.

A small pond indeed. This television station needed me, I could see that. It was the first and only TV station in town–the perfect environment for a growing fish like me. Work was plentiful.

Mary and I sensed that we could be happy here. Soon our two daughters would be followed by a son, Jeff. In this little hamlet we could raise our children, root ourselves, and fulfill our dreams.

If nothing got in the way.

Terrie, Jeffery, and Cindy.

Don and Mary.

* * *

My work as a media voice required high motivation, and I naturally gravitated toward books on the subject, along with all its offshoots: positive thinking, success orientation, self-actualization. With Mary by my side, I sat in seminars, listened to cassettes, attended rallies, read books. We immersed ourselves in a whole new circle of vivacious friends, people with glittery eyes and toothy smiles and warm, friendly handshakes. We came to believe in the magic of believing in ourselves.

When we first heard about direct home marketing—we knew it was the thing for us. Here was a method for putting teeth into our motivational concepts and positive thinking beliefs—and money in our pockets. We could discover the joys and riches of supplementing our income, and at the same time practice our preaching. We soon built a thriving home business.

Haw, this is a cinch! I said to myself one day as I balanced the business checkbook. The next morning I walked into the station and submitted my resignation.

* * *

Religion in this circle of people was a trendy thing. The traditional faiths were out—passé. We had never been enamored of the old-fashioned Christian stuff anyway—it didn't show me much, really. And yet, we felt a certain need, somewhere inside ourselves, to have a faith, a system of beliefs.

Our friends in the business were students of a new religion that mixed the goodness of Christianity with a westernized brand of eastern mysticism, communicating with God-words that seemed acceptable to people

40

from Christian backgrounds. Under the heady influence of our successful friends, we sought out this new religion. I liked it.

It was there that I learned what I had suspected all along: there really is no hell, they said, and no Satan, and no evil. There is really only goodness, peace, and heaven. After all, I reasoned with them, how could a good and loving God allow evil in the world He created? Preposterous.

It all made simple sense to Mary and me. We became devout and faithful believers. We said all the prayers–some were quite poetic–and called ourselves Christians, since we figured we were. All was well.

There was plenty of experimentation. Spiritualism, for example, was fascinating. And we were, after all, mature and intelligent adults. Everything was open for consideration and investigation. Besides, that little gnawing, that nervous sensation of need, was never quite satisfied. We dabbled with ouija boards and hypnotism, we played with palm-reading and Rosicrucianism, we studied astro-projection, extra-sensory perception, astrology. Along with our friends, we tried to contact the spirit world. Since the Bible declares that man is also a spirit, we reasoned, what was the harm in expanding our consciousness into the spiritual areas? Nobody was getting hurt, and–you had to admit–it was fascinating stuff. And there was that tiny, relentless, begging sense of need.

But we were making it big. And all through our own initiative! How could life be finer?

* * *

Then, suddenly, our lives were chaos. Within weeks of my resignation from the station, our sales arrived at a sudden plateau and stubbornly refused to climb. With the bi-weekly television paycheck gone, there was no source of regular income. The checkbook scraped bottom, and then some. I borrowed a little to get by, hoping things would improve. They didn't. I borrowed more, then still more. Every time I thought about the situation, the molars clenched reflexively in the back of my mouth. I was angry. But I would not give in. It was against my positive-thinking principles.

Mary was grim but just as dogged as I was. We clung to our sense of self-determination, convinced that somehow positive thinking would bail us out. Big fish or no, we were sinking in our own little pond.

Still, we were staunch adherents of our new found religion. It had not failed us. We must have—somehow —failed ourselves. By the religious logic we had learned there, this was the only explanation.

I returned, bitterly, to odd jobs, here and there, wherever I could get the work. Our debt grew deeper. Life became sullen.

My father suffered a fatal heart attack in November 1959. My mother tried to cope, but wasn't doing well. Since there was nothing to keep us in Traverse City, we trudged westward to Nebraska—to help her.

Life dragged on, from month to month, from year to year, as we carried our debts along. Finally, late in 1966

—seven years after leaving broadcasting—we moved back to Traverse City. I hung my head and walked into a Traverse City radio station to ask for work. The chit-chat skills took over instinctively. I got the job. We moved back to Traverse immediately.

I soon discovered that the ticket to success was not in TV or radio programs but in the commercials between them. Stardom was too elusive; a good salesman could gather quite a bit of grain into the barn. The more you got, the more you could go out and get! I decided to sell the one commodity that nobody else was selling: commercial time on Traverse City's fledgling television station.

Easy Street was once again in sight.

* * *

When Mary and I attended a positive thinking seminar at Northwestern Michigan College in Traverse City one day that fall, we had no idea that our spiritual lives would take a new twist as a result. The speaker and leader of the group called "Science of Enlightenment for the New Age" had a captivating presence, and everything he said was intriguing to me. I could tell this was a step beyond the toy-mysticism. It represented more intense, more organized beliefs—a true system of thought. There was more of a challenge to it, more of a thrill. I felt the same delight in it that I had felt years before, in the Orient, as I picked up bits and pieces of Eastern thought.

Soon Mary and I were driving out to the edge of town to attend meetings on their huge acreage. We obtained the services of our own guru, and drank deeply of meditation and contemplation. At long last, we felt we had found Divine Truth.

It paid off fast. Soon I was raking in the sales at the station, paying off one debt after another. I won the Bahamas trip in the station's sales incentive program. Our family life was good. Terrie and Cindy were grown and married to fine husbands. Jeff seemed to be well adjusted, not involved with drugs and such. We were able to put some money in the bank, then some more, and then a lot more. It felt like true self-actualization and success. If there was such a thing as nirvana—and I felt sure there must be—then this must be the great American version of it!

For now.

* * *

There were eighty wooded acres for sale just outside Traverse City—Jeff spotted the ad in the classifieds—and as soon as I saw it, I knew it was what we wanted. Our own place. A place to live out our golden years. Secluded, wooded Michigan. Perfect.

The group hated it, of course. They had their own secluded, wooded, perfect acreage, and they liked their adherents to locate on their property, commune-style. Mary and I were a little too independent for that. I didn't see any real conflict between aligning ourselves with the group and achieving our own personal goals. But such a land purchase stuck in their craw.

Soon Mary noticed we were failing to get news of SENA meetings and events, being left out of this and that. The strain crept into various relationships, until we found ourselves out there less and less, and treated more and more like outsiders when we were there.

But I was thrilled. We purchased the parcel on a land contract in the late summer of 1974, and I filled my mind with plans to build the house of our dreams. They could take a flying leap, as far as I was concerned. I had what I wanted.

We had no idea of the forces that were at work in our midst.

* * *

Our daughter Cindy had never been inclined toward the group. By the time we began to get involved there, she was already nearly engaged, soon to be married. So she had other concerns. Beside, the whole thing gave her the creeps. She had attended a few lectures, which had thoroughly convinced her of reincarnation as a fact —but one evening during one of the lectures, she began to feel an eerie presence in the auditorium. Driving home with a girlfriend, Cindy suddenly seemed to feel herself lose control of the car to an invisible force—which proceeded to drive the car home. Adequately frightened, Cindy stopped going to the meetings. And soon she was married and gone, past worrying about such things.

Terrie, on the other hand, was enamored with the leader. There was something magnetic about him, something compelling, something that commanded Terrie's attention. She became truly dedicated to him, and in fact, she and her husband did some public relations work for him after they relocated to Toronto. The concept of life as a collection of energies suited Terrie and Bob just fine.

It was young Jeff who had the struggle. From our earliest association with the group, Jeff hated to go to the meetings. He grew fidgety in the car as we approached the property. He was uncomfortable sitting in the meetings. He sneered at the leader with a penchant for selling a book or cassette or some other product at the end of each meeting, but Jeff's annoyance went deeper than that. As he sat in the sessions, trying to fill his mind with other things, he could sense cold evil at play in the air.

And, as the rest of us aligned our minds with the universe, Jeff–alone–could hear the frantic squealing of pigs.

3.

It Gets Worse

TERRIE sat up straight in bed, sweating. Her eyes were wide open, filled with the flames of a rampaging dream. She had seen a house–a house she had never seen before–explode into a boiling firestorm.

And she knew it was the home of her parents.

Mary smiled a little patronizingly as she listened to her oldest child describe the nightmare on the phone from Toronto. Mary was a seasoned mother, a woman who had come to allow for such occasional impulses on the part of her children. The dream, of course, meant nothing. It was silly. But Terrie needed to get it off her chest.

The contractors had already begun work, anyway. Don and Mary were excited. Each day they drove past the property to see progress. What a thrill, to watch our very own American dream come true!

And yet there were problems. As they tried to break ground, the builders broke three bulldozer blades in a row. The earth was not supposed to be that hard here. There was little real rock to speak of. Nothing had ever been built on the land.

When Terrie heard about the incidents, she was more sure than ever that the land was sick. The sense of foreboding lingered with her. But her parents would not hear her.

The work hobbled forward. Deer season came, claiming the entire construction crew without warning. Don, irritated, watched the land sit idle for weeks. It was already late fall. Once the men returned, materials were unavailable, and unexplainably so. Delays became costly.

On the Monday morning after Thanksgiving, the phone rang. Mary picked it up.

"Why hasn't my husband been paid for his work?" the wife of one of the contractor's workers demanded. Mary's mouth turned down instinctively.

"I have no idea," she responded. "I'll look into it right away."

Within hours, Don and Mary had poked their fingers into a gooey spider's web of intrigue. Before they could nab him, the contractor had panicked and run. He disappeared—with the money—somewhere in Canada.

Shaken, Don and Mary trudged through the forlorn house. The exterior was only half completed. The cold blasts were already pushing their way down from the

48

north country. The Brubakers had already sold the house they were living in at present; now they had nowhere to go. Through an attorney, he begged the buyers to rent them their own house till spring.

They sat at the kitchen table over coffee and shook their heads. Presumably, if they were to believe all they had been led to believe, this was all for their good. But it certainly tasted bad. These troubles might be part of some cosmic design, something to help them grow strong, as part of their "karma." But they were tired of being troubled, tired of growing the hard way.

Resolutely, they pieced together their situation. The contractor, they convinced themselves, would be caught and brought to justice. The bankers had been wrong in the way they had issued the loan, allowing the contractor too much freedom in spending. The bankers should likewise be liable. In the meantime, Don and Mary reasoned, they had a roof over their heads–if only a rented one–Don's income was good, and everything would work out eventually. They were human beings, after all, and they could cling to that.

The winter roared through. The legal process seemed frozen over. As spring peeked in, the buyer of the Brubaker's house demanded that they vacate.

Irritated, Don decided the logical thing to do would be to put a mobile home on the land near the uncompleted house. For days, the family moved load after back-breaking load of belongings from the rented house in the city to the mobile home on the outskirts of town. Squeeze, condense, cram, discard. Six rooms of furnishings packed into a fourteen-by-seventy aluminum tube. Don growled at his luck. Things had to improve with the springtime. Almost hour by hour, he worked to keep his outlook positive.

It was, after all, peaceful and quiet on their property. In the evenings, after the day's work, he could relax and feel as if things were going to work out. The summertime would give them all a chance to work on the house themselves. Positive thinking would pull them through.

On Memorial Day 1975, Don and Jeff unloaded the last truckload of stuff–the last of the heirlooms, the last of the antiques, the last of the appliances–and sighed a collective sigh of relief. Mary had been slaving to keep pace with them, arranging things inside the mobile home as they dumped them off hour after hour. Now, with the end in sight, they were tired and hungry.

The hamburger place in Maple City suddenly sounded very good.

It was a festive moment, relatively speaking, so they let the whimpering dog come along, even though they normally left him behind. They all piled into the car and roared away, satisfied that they had pulled off such a monster of a job.

It felt great to sit down, even on hard formica booth seats, and savor the aroma of ground beef and other delights. They had, in a way, beaten the present at its own game, and could once again get on with their future. Don enjoyed the sense of private, thorough satisfaction.

None of them thought anything about it when a flurry of fire trucks went by the hamburger place, racing east toward Traverse City.

* * *

The gas line leaked, silently. Invisible gas covered the floor, then filled up the mobile home like a huge bathtub. Meanwhile, the pilot light flickered innocently in the gas stove in the kitchen, waiting for fuel.

When the gas had inched up to the level of the pilot light, the mobile home became a massive bomb. Detonation was instantaneous and complete. Everything was annihilated in a single, horrible moment. Nearby residents saw the roof blow forty feet into the air, the explosion rocking walls and china cabinets a mile away.

The Brubakers were driving leisurely back from Maple City when Jeff spotted the column of rusty black smoke making the sky ugly over their corner of the horizon. Don felt a momentary pulse in his stomach, and drove faster, even as he tried to tell himself how absurd such a thought really was.

As they rounded the curve a quarter-mile from their home, the three of them stared blankly at the inferno. It was like footage from a bad movie, unconvincing because of its extremity. The black, twisted base of the mobile home was gushing flames, as if it had opened a direct line to hell. Nothing from inside the mobile home —no furniture, no appliance, no heirloom—could be distinguished. There was only fire, and blackened carnage.

Fire trucks had already converged on the scene, and hapless firemen were shooting pitiful little streams of water into the furnace. Mary nearly fell from the car, stunned. She dropped to her knees, and began pounding the Michigan earth with vengeance.

"No more!" she sobbed. "No more! We can't stand anymore!"

Don helped her up, silently, as her shoulders convulsed and her wailing grew unintelligible. Jeff stood alone, unable to move, unable to comprehend the event.

The teeth in the back of Don's mouth ground together furiously. He had snapped. Somebody–anybody –was going to pay.

In Toronto, Terrie felt a strange little quirk in the pit of her stomach. <u>Wonder how Mom and Dad are doing? . . .</u>

* * *

The insurance company dragged its feet on the claim for the destroyed mobile home. Don began exacting his revenge immediately. He authorized his lawyer to sue the insurance company, along with the former contractor, and to throw in a suit against the mobile home manufacturer–and everybody else connected with the faulty gas line, too.

The thirst for vindication began to consume him. Day by day he grew more manic. His family became uncomfortable around him. At the station, the other staffers found it difficult to work with him. Finally the station manager asked Don to resign. Don refused, determining to go down fighting. The firing happened. Don left seething.

Chafing under legal threats, the insurance company put the Brubakers up in an apartment while the suit dragged on. Don also harassed the bank into lending him enough money to finish construction on the house —while that lawsuit, too, wound its way through the courts. With no work—and needing none, for the time being—Don had plenty of time on his hands for personally supervising the completion of the house. Meanwhile he could pursue the lawsuit against the manufacturer of the mobile home. In an insidious way, it gave him a sense of pleasure to strangle those creeps who had created such havoc in his well-planned life.

Mary, too, in her own way, was caught up in the tension of it all. To handle it, she just gulped a few good drinks in the evening, after the day's work was done, and a couple more if Don were late getting home, and perhaps a nightcap with him after his arrival. She could stare a bottle down just about as well as the next lady. In fact, if the truth were known, Mary was just about as alcoholic as anybody could be. Except for slumming in the gutter, which a lady does not do. Mary could slum right here in this lousy rented apartment, in her living room, or her kitchen. And with Don only a few drinks behind her, why not?

Jeff watched the subtle transformation in his parents, and was disgusted. The pressures were on at school. His peers were after him. Some days he just felt sick of everything . . .

53

The lawyers assured the Brubakers that if they won any one of their various lawsuits, they would have enough money to live comfortably for the rest of their days. It was the Good Life. Enjoy it, Mary. Enjoy it, Don.

* * *

There was a rather silly little program on television—Mary couldn't even recall how she first came to run across it. A religious program, with a preacher and his wife hosting what looked like a talk show. It was funny at first to Mary, but she took to watching the ninety minutes each afternoon when it came on, and was soon hooked. There was laughter and conversation and good diversion from the dullness of her long, lonely drinking sprees. Some days she was able to get more out of the program than others. It made her feel good. And she wanted to feel good.

Some of it, of course, warmed her nostalgically. They prayed on this program, for example. You could call them—they were on the air live in some cities, although Mary wasn't sure when and where—and you could tell them what you wanted them to pray with you about. Mary recalled her childhood, which somehow had seemed to be an innocent, less complicated time, a time when saying prayers had made her feel better, no matter what juvenile trial she might be facing. In reality, her life had been troubled and broken. As the youngest of three sisters, she had stood in a courtroom in Iowa and looked in the face of a judge who was trying to decide which parent would get which daughters.

"Would you rather live with your mother or your father?" he intoned.

Mary pouted. "If I can't have them both," she replied, "I don't want either one of them."

Mary's mother had galloped into the sunset, eventually marrying seven times. Mary stubbornly loved her anyway–she found her fascinating and in many ways even admirable. Still, Mary's face burned every time she heard people talking about "that woman."

The judge had placed Mary with her hard-shelled Baptist grandmother, who would not sleep in the same room as Grandpa. Mary's father lived nearby and stayed in close touch, and talked Grandma into letting Mary attend the First Christian Church in town, where he was personally more comfortable.

Mary had been baptized there, to please her dad, to please herself. She wanted to feel accepted. She didn't know what it meant, but it felt right–especially compared to the overwhelming wrongness she felt whenever she looked at her splintered family.

And now, years later, sitting in a drunken fog, watching a smiley TV preacher pray for her on her television set, Mary felt that same vague sense of right, that same odd longing to distance herself from the wrongs she felt had crowded in around her. The group hypocrites had left her angry. The success drive was unraveling her life thread by thread now–it didn't feel like the be-all end-all she had expected it to be. High-powered positive thinking didn't really cut it for her. When she looked at her reflection in the amber bottle before her, she could see everything she wasn't–and only this crazy little ninety-minute wedge of time each day, this strange daily encounter with Christianity, seemed to be bolstering her at all.

Those people, on TV–the people that Mary watched each day on that program–they had something she wanted, something she didn't see when she looked at her haggard reflection in the glass of a bottle of beer. It was something that they had that the group had never even approached. But exactly what it was, she couldn't tell.

She was confused. They had been taught that only peace and goodness existed, that evil was an illusion. Yet evil persisted, invading their lives at every turn. The group had taken them into divine mysticism, a "oneness" with the world and universe. And yet, Mary felt more fragmented than ever. Christianity, of course, was outmoded–she knew that. And yet, she was so, so unhappy . . .

On an empty day, Mary sat bewildered in front of the TV set, fighting back tears of despair. The drinking was making her sick, and the sickness was making her drink. She could not latch onto a single moment of joy. Every new thought was grim.

As she watched the program, she felt her insides swell with remorse. Her eyes swelled with tears, and she slipped uncontrollably out of the chair and onto her knees.

"God!" she cried out, anguished. "Take me, or take my drinking!"

She could scarcely tell what had made her say such a thing. But as she blinked, Mary felt her mind clearing instantly. She looked at the bottle and the glass. They repulsed her. She picked herself up and emptied them both into the sink, with no sense of regret.

Mary did not discuss the incident with Don. She would not learn until much later that, ironically, Don had put the program on the air in Traverse City himself, when none of the other station salespeople would talk to the "religious fanatics." Mary wouldn't know what to say to Don, anyway. It was as strange to her as it would have been to him. Somehow, God seemed to be at work in her life—or in their lives—or something. But she couldn't come close to piecing it all together.

She never drank again.

* * *

His emotional muscles taut and his eyes still fiery, Don Brubaker moved his wife and son into their dream house in December of 1975. Revenge was sweet. Now—finally—the cross country skiing, the quiet, the long hours of solitude could mellow him. He had done it himself. As always.

Soon Don needed money again. Unemployment checks were not covering their expenses—and Don wanted to live a finer life than this. Their savings were growing dangerously low. He knew he needed to be productive. And broadcasting was such a natural part of him . . .

Setting aside his pride, Don mended the relationship at the television station and went back to work as a super-salesman. All the old instincts, the old positive thinking, the old "karma," were quick to click again. He motivated himself into a frenetic pace of successful selling. His emotional system began whirring away again.

For a year, he pushed. Pushing paid off. Don's sales increased steadily through the winter. The holiday season brought its annual round of parties. The new house was a thorough joy, a wonderful launching pad for all the social stuff the Brubakers were going to do. And they did it all. Mary coyly avoided alcohol, but other than that slight aberration, the year-end festivities were full of fun.

It looked like 1977 would be their best year ever.

* * *

When Jeff awoke and left for school, Mary began to rouse, groggy at first. The New Year was less than a week old, and she was not yet in the routine of normal daily activity again. The party schedule had thrown her body clock off, and now she needed a little extra time to get going in the morning.

Don, of course, was long gone. He was already gunning for big money in the New Year, having spent a couple days up north hustling new business. What a dynamo, Mary mused. Sometimes just thinking about his pace wore her out.

She plodded toward the shower and twisted the knobs for HOT and COLD. Her thoughts flowed together as the water covered her. What a strange amalgam of memories! Brutal, demoralizing pain—mixed with certain and sweet joys. Life had indeed been bittersweet for her in the past year. She smiled and sighed, somehow satisfied.

Mary left the damp towel neatly folded on the rack and pulled on a pair of everyday slacks and a simple top. Maybe she would run into town today and pick up a few things. And yes, she needed to call Cindy down in Plainwell–Cindy and her husband needed a washing machine, so Mary and Don were going to send one down. Their little grandson, Ryan, after all, was pushing three months old, and going through diapers like crazy!

After a little bit of long-distance chit-chat with Cindy, Mary assembled some breakfast, thumbed through the ad section of yesterday's newspaper, and was just beginning to rinse her coffee cup when the phone rang.

"Mrs. Brubaker?"

"Yes."

"I'm calling from the Osteopathic emergency room," the woman said. "Your husband would like you to pray for him."

"What's wrong," Mary demanded, spitting the words through her teeth. "What's happened?"

"Don is having a heart attack–"

All the alarms went off in Mary's mind. She could not hear any more.

"God . . . God . . . God . . ." she muttered, breathing hard.

4.

Trip Number One

A winter storm has blown up, as if to salt yet another fresh wound. Visibility is very poor and the roads have become extremely hazardous. Mary is too frantic to drive. She calls the State Police. All of their units are tied up dealing with the snowy mess out there.

Mary stops to think, trying not to let her mind go careening out of control. Shirley, a neighbor, lives only a half mile away. Maybe she will help. Mary dials the number, stiffening her fingers to keep from shaking. Moments later, Mary is hurrying through the icy wind toward Shirley's car.

Don lies bare-chested on a table, still in the emergency room, surrounded by personnel and equipment and tubes and wires. Mary catches her breath as she looks at her husband, lying quiet. She finds herself silently reciting old prayers, as she stares, hopeless.

The light of God surrounds me. The presence of God watches over me. The power of God protects me. Wherever I am, God is. The light of God surrounds me ....

Dr. Douglas introduces Mary to Dr. Benjamin—"the best there is," he says—and then turns her over to a nurse for safekeeping.

"But why can't I stay with Don?" Mary demands, snapping out of her reverie. "Can't I be with my husband?"

"Walk with us to the elevator," the doctor offers, "but we really do need some information from you about Don."

Mary clings to her husband's cold hand as they move down the corridor. Don lies silent, motionless. Bob follows nearby. At the elevator, a nurse touches Mary's arm and guides her aside to an office. As they turn away together, Don's body suddenly lurches. Mary's head snaps toward her husband, but the nurse tightens her grip. The elevator doors close on Don and the medical team.

"Get him up to C.C.U., stat!" Mary hears someone say inside the elevator car. "We're gonna need the paddles."

Mary dumps herself into a chair and sobs. Bob stands near, unable to help, unable to speak any consolation.

The nurse begins her litany of questions. Don's background. His health. His habits. Mary answers mechanically, unable to concentrate on anything but the awful mental picture of her husband heaving and convulsing somewhere above her.

Mary sits still as long as she can, then begs a moment from the nurse to use a telephone. Her mind is whirling. She wants to get help—any help. She dials an old leader from the group and asks her to pray. She assures her that she will pray for Don.

Back in her antiseptic cubicle, information is scarce. The nurse can give Mary no news about Don. No doctor reports back. Each minute hangs like rotting fruit, waiting to splatter.

"I want to see Dr. Benjamin," Mary finally insists.

"I'll see what I can do," the nurse responds.

The doctor appears a few moments later. Don is being well taken care of, he assures her, and she can see him in a few moments.

"I think you should call your family," the doctor advises gently. "Don's condition is quite serious."

Mary looks at the doctor through empty, tired eyes, then picks herself up and trudges toward a phone. She calls Terrie in Toronto—she isn't in; husband Bob takes the message—and Cindy downstate, and leaves a message for Jeff at school. She calls Don's mother. Then she calls the television station and a few friends. With each new call, the trauma is revisited upon her. Each person reacts with fresh horror to the awful news. By the time Mary is done with the chore, she is overwhelmed with weariness.

Finally she is ushered into the awful room where a crowd of doctors and nurses has been slaving over Don's limp form. Now, most of them have done their biggest job—keeping him alive for the time being. Machines have taken over now. Don seems to be attached to hundreds of tubes and wires, a pale mannequin. He is not entirely unconscious, but his words are rubbery. Mary sits by his side until he drifts to sleep. Then the night nurse leads her to a cot in the next room, where Mary pushes her shoes off and lies down, rigid, frightened.

The pages of her mental scrapbook inevitably begin to unfurl. She hasn't seen Don in a hospital since 1948, the year he hurt his back in the car accident and proposed marriage to her. The doctors said he'd never walk again. She knew better. Look at what he has made of himself since then!

What was it, she wonders, that attracted her to him back then? His nose. Yes, it was his nose. A beautiful Roman nose. And he was big and handsome. He looked like a protector, a source of security and safety. She wanted that so badly.

She felt safe in his arms on their wedding night. They talked late into the night about their future, and their family. They were anxious to have children. Nine months and three days after their wedding, in fact, Terrie was born. What a giddy, fulfilling year, knowing that joy, that comfort.

Now Mary feels far away from Don, vulnerable and alone. Her children are distant, racing from their various distractions to join their mother—but after the fact. Mary Brubaker's husband lies clinging to life, alone.

She aches for sleep.

* * *

Jeff senses something is amiss even as he approaches the house. The dog is whining. Mom is not home. Someone—it isn't Mom's handwriting—has left a note on the table: "Pack your things. Your dad went for a test. Somebody will pick you up."

Bob pulls into the driveway. Jeff is full of questions.

It was a heart attack, Bob concedes.

Jeff instinctively jumps to the obvious conclusion.

<u>He's dead,</u> he hears his mind declare silently.

By the time they reach the hospital, hysteria has overcome him. Four men hold him still as Mary tries to calm him in the waiting room. He finally disintegrates into a quaking shambles.

* * *

Terrie picks up the telephone to hear her mother sounding unlike her mother. Mary is hysterical, terrified that Don is dying.

Terrie is deeply frightened, but something tells her, immediately, that her mother is wrong. Her father, Terrie knows, will pull through.

So she summons up all the courage she can, and—digging into her teachings—consoles her mother by telling her to dwell on the color purple. Thinking about colors is important to their philosophy.

She assures her mother she will get on the first available flight.

Her first sight of her father is a sickening one. He has deflated, and is shriveled into a sickly heap. She is not used to hospitals anyway, and the white walls and white sheets engulf his white face—and make his beard stand out, giving him a ghostly appearance.

Terrie feels her life-force flowing out of her. She figures her father must be drawing energy from those around him. That is how she understands things to happen.

But it seems as if no amount of energy can ever hope to energize him. He looks like such a frail little thing.

* * *

Something terrible shoots through Cindy's body the moment she hears her mother's voice on the phone. She just talked with Mom this morning—it's not like her to call twice in one day.

"Where's Jim?" Mary asks, sounding distraught.

Jim is at night school. It will be an hour before he gets home. But Cindy doesn't answer her mother. "What's wrong?" she responds.

"Your father's had a heart attack."

The rest of the conversation runs together in a blur. When Cindy hangs up, the shock takes over, and she sits silently for the full hour, holding baby Ryan, and waiting for her husband to come home.

Then, when Jim is there to hold her, the shock wears off. And Cindy cries, hard.

The little family drives north toward Traverse City the next morning. The snowstorm has left towering snow banks on either side of the road, and to Cindy they seem higher, more threatening, than she has ever seen.

Her father's face seems over-sized against the white linens. Cindy approaches quietly, along his left side, and waits for his eyes to open. When they do, Don smiles at her.

"How were the roads?" he asks weakly. He sounds casual, but he looks frightened.

Cindy feels strange. It is a look she has never seen in him before.

He was always her rock. . . .

* * *

Outside the hospital, an out-of-towner is driving by. He happens to be heading home after a day of errands in Traverse City. He pastors the Assembly of God church up in Boyne City.

Suddenly, inexplicably, as he passes the hospital, he feels impressed to pray for Don Brubaker.

He has only met Don twice—and both times were quite a while ago. Once, the pastor was trying to get some television coverage for evangelistic crusades in Boyne City. Another time, he visited the station with some representatives from the religious program who were trying to get their show on the Traverse City station—and all the station personnel fled before the "religious fanatics" got there, except for affable Don Brubaker, who could enjoy a conversation with virtually anybody.

Why, then, the pastor wonders, does he feel impressed to pray for the TV salesman—now, after all this time?

The pastor obediently prays as he drives on, without knowing why. The next day he drops a card in the mail to Don Brubaker, mentioning the little incident and generally inquiring about Don. Mary reads the card —and she knows God is at work.

* * *

The night nurse, Debbie, is a fresh-scrubbed, innocent new grad from nursing school. It is an honor for her to have been assigned to C.C.U., the coronary care unit. She finds a new patient when she arrives that evening.

The doctors, she learns from other nurses, give Don Brubaker very little chance of survival.

Debbie makes her usual rounds, then settles behind the desk with a cup of coffee. Occasionally she glances at Don's monitor, but he seems to be holding his own. After three quiet hours on the floor, Debbie feels things might go smoothly the entire shift.

She jumps as the monitor's insistent beeping cuts through the silence. Debbie's eyes lock on the screen: Don's heart is fibrillating, beating wildly, desperate to pump more oxygen to his system. Doctors and nurses flash into the area from all over the hospital, converging on the tiny cubicle where Don Brubaker lies.

The commotion has roused Mary Brubaker, and

Debbie sees her moving sleepily into the hall, her face painted with alarm. For a moment, Debbie wants to go to her, to comfort her – but the patient is beginning to thrash in his bed. Debbie's eyes move back to Don, and then grow wide. In her short career, she has not encountered anything like this. His body is writhing and twisting, he is calling out, as if the hospital were a battlefield. Nurses are leaning over him, putting their weight on his shoulders to keep him horizontal.

"Satan!" the patient cries out suddenly–and for a split-second, everything in the room falls silent–"Get behind me and stay there!"

Debbie feels a shiver run through her body. Nursing school has not prepared her for such a spectacle. She knows of no drugs that would cause such a reaction. As she stands, her eyes riveted on the panicky scene, she wonders what is happening inside the mind of that desperate man.

On the outer edges of the scene, Mary Brubaker stands, unbelieving, horrified. Debbie notices her. <u>Someone should get her out of here,</u> she says to herself. Then, as she watches, Mary's face turns darker. Debbie looks back at Don. He is fighting with more energy, pushing away at everything around him. But as Debbie looks into his face, she feels a deep chill. His eyes are bulging, his teeth showing like an animal's. His face is full of fear, as if her were staring into the face of torture itself. As the monitor screams, Don snarls and snorts and gnashes his teeth. Debbie's body is rigid as she watches the team labor over him–and against him.

Long afterward, as the crisis passes and the team filters away into other corners of the hospital, Debbie can still feel the tension inside her.

* * *

As Don convulses and fights to sit up, Mary wants to turn away. But she keeps watching, with a sick sadness stewing in her gut. Occasionally he will speak, but he is not coherent. He almost appears to be wrestling with an invisible opponent.

As she watches Don writhe on the bed, Mary is horrified by the transformation that sweeps across his face. Momentarily his features take on a contorted, demonic expression. What is happening to her husband?

Finally the nurses and doctors calm Don, and he falls asleep, heavily sedated. Mary goes back to her cot and lies down, unable to sleep. Instinctively, she knows something more awful than just a heart attack is happening to Don. But what is it?

Who is he fighting?

The battle, so brief and furious, is only now beginning. Don Brubaker will spend months and months lying in that bed–and there are more nights of torture to come.

* * *

Veteran Bertha has padded around this place in her white rubber soles for seventeen years. She comes on duty the morning after Don is admitted just as she has come on duty every morning. She has no inkling, as Debbie and others brief her about the patients in the ward, that she has turned a final corner in her life.

The chart on Don Brubaker, in its physical form, looks and feels just like thousands of others Bertha has handled in her long career. But as her eyes absorb the numbers and letters, and run along the scraggly lines that the monitors have so relentlessly traced out through the night, a vague sense of foreboding settles into her stomach. This man, she realizes immediately, is intensely sick. The chances of him living through her shift are slim indeed. Bertha glances over at the paste-faced gentleman. The odds are that he will be a corpse by nightfall. Bertha glances back down at his chart, and her eyes fall upon the blank labeled "age." Don Brubaker is exactly as old as she is. Bertha sighs. It could be her in that bed instead of him.

She grew up in a Christian home, and with a strong sense of knowing that there is life after death. The concept really hit home when her young marriage was shattered by the intrusion of death: her husband died suddenly at the age of thirty-four.

It had been a complex time for Bertha. A faithful churchgoer throughout her childhood and teens, she had felt strange when she and her husband had grown slack in their church attendance. Her husband had never professed a faith in Christ, which worried her. Then, suddenly, this devastating illness. Bertha stewed forlornly as she sat by his sleeping form in the hospital. If he died–what would become of him?

The pastor came to visit, and while he was there, Bertha's husband stirred. Bertha looked at him anxiously. He was utterly peaceful, a radiant calm filling his face. He opened his eyes.

"It's beautiful over there," he said quietly.

Then he died.

"See, Bertha?" the pastor said gently. "You've been worrying for nothing."

Now, years later, Bertha stands next to the sleeping form of another dying man. She clutches his chart, thinking back through that brush with death so long ago. She can't help but wonder what is going on inside the head—and heart—of this fellow.

* * *

"Dr. Hart," the voice crackles over the hospital intercom. "Dr. Hart."

It is a thin disguise for an emergency. Instantly, all personnel connected with coronary care rush to C.C.U. Someone is dying.

Lynn comes hurrying with the rest. A transplanted New Yorker, she is among the toughest nurses on the floor. She often takes charge when no doctors are immediately on hand, pounding on a patient's chest to restore his heartbeat, or administering the electric paddles, sending huge bolts of electricity through the body.

"It's Don again," she says as a doctor comes running. "He's going into V-tach."

Don Brubaker has been on the floor for five days, and already he has caused more of an uproar than any patient in memory. His condition, so delicate, so dangerous, never seems to stabilize for more than a few hours at a time. Then, it is always another crisis. Each one looks like a killer.

Lynn is secretly amazed that Don Brubaker is still alive.

The doctor starts a Dilantin drip. Sometimes the drug will calm a fibrillating heart. Lynn watches the monitor intensely. No change. She injects Lidocaine, the only other drug that has any hope of helping. It doesn't work either. Suddenly, inevitably, Don heaves and falls unconscious.

"We've got to defib him," the doctor says. "Get the paddles ready." Lynn hooks up the instruments and hands them to the doctor. "Everyone clear," he orders, leaning over the patient and pressing the paddles against his chest.

Boom! The bolt of power jolts Don's body, causing him to arch as if he has been slammed by a cement truck. The monitor falls silent. Don's heart has shut down.

The team administers the standard C.P.R. routine, pounding on Don's chest in the prescribed manner. Nurses keep the medications flowing into his system, struggling to get his heart to unlock and begin beating again.

Lynn eyes the monitor. No change. Boom! Another bolt, another jump. Lynn looks into the monitor screen, hoping against hope to see it spring to life. But no change.

More medication. The doctor is sweating now. Each minute stretches like chewing gum around the clock. Five minutes, ten minutes, fifteen—Lynn knows that it could all be over soon. No human being can live after a quarter-hour interruption of his heartbeat. The loss of circulation to the brain alone will render a survivor a complete vegetable. Still they slave away over him. Twenty minutes stretches to thirty, then to thirty-five, then to forty. The faces of the medical team are hot and grim. This looks like a sure loser.

Clinically, Don Brubaker is already dead.

Lynn is startled when the monitor suddenly begins beeping rhythmically again. The entire team looks up reflexively at the monitor, as if it has somehow mal-functioned. No patient in this hospital has ever been gone for forty-five minutes—not like this—and survived.

Lynn's body relaxes slightly after the long haul. This Don Brubaker, if he makes it, is going to have quite a story to tell. But he can hardly be expected to make it, Lynn tells herself. His odds are exceedingly long.

She wipes a line of perspiration from her upper lip and looks at the patient.

<u>Let's not do this again, Don, okay?</u> she thinks.

* * *

When Lynn visits Don the next time, he is conscious. "You had another rough time of it, Don," she says gently.

"I know," he replies weakly. "You gave me Dilantin and Lidocaine, and they didn't work, did they?"

Lynn looks at him in shock. Don was completely unconscious during the sparring match with his stubborn heart. There is no way he could have been aware of what was going on around him.

Lynn quizzes him in detail. Don answers every question with precise accuracy—the drugs, the procedures, even the conversations between the doctors and nurses.

A chill runs down Lynn's spine as Don tells her how he knows: He watched the episode from above the room, floating out of his body, looking down on his own lifeless form.

Lynn blinks and suppresses a sound. There is no viable explanation for this. Don knows too much too well. She tries to concoct some other rationale—he has read a book about similar experiences, or he has seen a movie. But no. His recollection of the events in the room is as clear as Lynn's own.

And she knows that none of the drugs could have caused hallucinations. Don's story, even so, would not qualify as a hallucination. It is too accurate. It is the truth!

This is a very unusual man.

5.

Trip Number Two

A S the doctors wheeled me into the elevator, everything suddenly went dark. It felt as if my cart fell out from under me.

I opened my eyes. Instead of being inside an elevator, I was inside a dark tunnel. My stomach knotted instantly in fear. The air was damp, cold, and musty. And I felt my speed picking up dangerously.

There was a sudden <u>whoosh</u>, and I saw a large glowing red ball approaching me, almost like the light on the front of a train. In that instant, as the red ball rushed toward me, I knew terror like never before. As it approached, I realized that it was really a large, eerie red eye. It stopped when it got close to me, and then began traveling alongside me through the tunnel. I could hardly stand to look at it, its gaze was so piercing. It felt like it was looking right into my mind, into my very soul.

I struggled to grasp what was happening to me, and all so fast. Only a moment ago Mary had been holding my hand, telling me everything was going to be all right. Now—mayhem.

Everything was happening so fast, I just wished I could focus for a moment. But there was no time for that. The red eye and I were still moving at incredible speeds, and everything around me was a blur of motion.

The sensation of speed was fantastic. It seemed as if I were moving downhill headfirst, even though I was on my back and I had the sensation of being able to see ahead of me, as if I were falling feet-first. But I couldn't begin to get a grasp on such details. The nightmare was consuming me far too fast.

Suddenly the tunnel was filled with a loud ringing, a sound that shook my entire body. It seemed as if the sound were piercing the very center of my being. My head began to throb. If I concentrated even for a moment, I could imagine a huge anvil being beaten rhythmically, mercilessly, by a monster blacksmith, just above my head. And the sound, though it seemed impossible, got louder and still louder.

Still I was plunging into the depths of this horrible tunnel.

Finally, after what seemed like long minutes, the ringing faded, and the tunnel—again, impossibly—got blacker as I continued to fall.

My throat was too thoroughly gripped by fear to scream. But I wanted to scream for help.

It was then, finally, that I looked down. I couldn't be sure even where "down" was, but as I looked there, I began to perceive that I was still in the hospital, in a room, in the middle of a circle of doctors and nurses. I glanced at the walls of the tunnel, walls of deep black whirring past me like video footage on fast forward. Yes, I was still there, still falling millions of miles into some terrible pit. And yet, there I was, lying deathlike on a hospital bed. I could see myself there, and it panicked me all the more.

My breath was coming in short bursts and my throat was burning like a forest fire. I could hear someone saying, "Try to breathe slower! Relax!" It was the voice of a doctor. But I couldn't get control. I couldn't stop breathing in explosions.

All at once pain flooded my senses. I felt literally torn apart, as if someone had begun slashing me to pieces with a samurai sword. In my mind, I could feel myself screaming–if only for relief. But I could not make myself scream.

Inexplicably, my incredible speed was finally, thankfully, tapering off. As I fought the horrible pain inside me, the scene around me slowed, until in a moment I was floating, suspended as if on an air cushion, in the musty tunnel. And the red eye, still alongside me, was staring ominously into my being.

The eye–suddenly I realized that I was seeing the hospital room through the red eye. It was absurd to me that I hadn't realized this before–and yet I could hardly process my thoughts. It was all too bizarre.

Twenty-four hours ago I was the model of typical American success! Now–this preposterous episode!

When I looked into the eye, I could see the doctors and nurses working over me, feverishly. Was I dying? Was I already dead? My mind raced, seeking some sense of order. Nothing was making sense. What was happening to me?

I was cold and scared. And I felt alone, more alone that I had ever felt in my forty-eight years. Almost physically, the sense of being cared for slipped away, and I felt the void as if it were a lump in my stomach. Nobody loved me. Instead, the sense of being unloved overwhelmed me like nausea.

"God!" I cried out, startling Mary and the nurses. "Doesn't anybody love me?"

Panic started building in my mind as it began to dawn on me where I was, suspended in this dank tube. As the red eye glowered at me, the thoughts began to arrange themselves, coalescing slowly. Suddenly, the idea was undeniable.

I was in hell.

The realization swept over me like an ocean wave, unstoppable though I tried desperately to dismiss it. Hell! I didn't even <u>believe</u> in hell! And here I was? This was it?

I had only the briefest moment to react to the thought when a deep, comfortable voice echoed through the tunnel.

"Have no fear, my son," the voice said with a certain resounding nobility, "for I am with you. I have chosen you to write about the experiences you will go through."

It was too unreal. I had never been given to believe in "missions from God" and the like anyway. And yet here was a voice that I knew was God's–sounding very much to me like John Carradine, the old character actor with the basso profuno voice–telling me I had been selected for this nightmare!

<u>This is silly!</u> my mind responded instantly. <u>I'm not a writer, I'm an advertising man. This can't really be happening!</u>

But the voice answered my doubting thoughts.

"I have chosen you," He said resolutely. "Don't be afraid. Believe me."

My being could not resist the power of the voice. There was something compelling in it that I was not prepared to override. I did believe.

"God <u>is</u> here!" I cried, surprising everyone in the hospital room once again–although I did not know it at the time.

I could feel my fears being chased away. I could feel myself relaxing for the first time since the incredible journey began.

<u>But if He is God, why is He here, in this darkness?</u>

Again, the voice responded to my unspoken doubts.

"You'll first experience hell," He said evenly, with a tone of complete control, "to prove to you the reality of evil. You've only believed that there was goodness. You must see for yourself that hell is real. And then you can tell others about the awful reality of hell, and about the beautiful glory of heaven."

Finally I had the nerve to speak up.

"But why me, God?"

"Because you represent common man," He responded. "You're not a noted minister or a highly educated theologian. People will more easily relate to and accept your story."

He sounded patient to me, although I felt very small before the voice.

"You will experience much in the months to come," the voice continued, "before you leave the hospital. But don't be afraid. You will live. You will recover. Nothing will harm you. And you will remember all that happens to you."

I did not have a chance to respond. I blinked without blinking–and as I did, everything disappeared. The next moment, Mary was beside me, among the doctors and nurses.

Fatigue washed over me suddenly, and I was annoyed by it. The doctor was explaining that I had suffered a severe heart attack. But that didn't really concern me. I wanted to tell Mary where I had been, what I had seen and heard. It was just that the fatigue pressed in on me, making conversation such hard work. . . .

"We've been wrong, Mary" I said, pushing the words out. "There is a hell. But even more important, Jesus is just as real. And God is with me now. He cares."

I could only force out a few words for each thought –and I was struggling even with this. Mary seemed to be listening, and I wanted to tell it all. Quick–before sleep.

Sleep was coming, I could tell. My mind was racing, but my body had already pulled in for a pit stop. I was filled with wonder about what had happened, and more than a little apprehension about what was coming up. I could almost taste the bitterness of hell–and yet I knew, instinctively, that I would drink more deeply of it in the days to come. Only when? How?

And still . . . why?

My apprehension gave way to a thorough, blanketing sense of protection. I knew I would be all right. I knew God would take care of me. His voice had convinced me. It might be hard–I had the idea it would be –but He had promised to take care of me.

As I relaxed and let sleep overtake me, I felt myself beginning to slip downhill again. I opened my eyes and found myself back in the tunnel, moving faster and faster. The darkness engulfed me once again, and the speed made me almost giddy.

In moments, I felt weightlessness. And my mind began to fill up with random, almost silly concerns. I hope I don't travel too far . . . I hope I can find my way back . . . I hope I can keep from being afraid, according to instructions . . .

Suddenly, my plunge ended, and I was dangling in mid-air, like a helium-filled balloon, a toy. Then, with no warning, beautiful white lights danced into view all around me.

The white light began pulsating, and with each pulse it changed into intense color. It was almost as if I were seeing everything through a prism. The colors had an awesome clarity and brilliance. The air was alive.

Slowly, the colors faded, and in their place was a placid springtime scene with gently rolling hills, luscious trees, a deep blue sky–so breathtaking that it almost demanded comment.

It's like paradise, I said to myself. It's so peaceful and tranquil! I felt as if I could be happy staying there forever.

But then, as I floated in the warm spring air, drinking in the incredible scenery, I began to sense another presence in the vicinity. I couldn't see anyone, but I knew someone was with me.

"You don't have to go through this pain, Don," the voice said, sweet and seductive. It was a slightly nasal voice, tainted with a whiny edge. The voice dripped with honey, yet it had a tinge of the sinister about it.

"Follow me," the voice went on, "and you can have everything you ever hoped for. Be the person I want you to be, and you can have everything you desire."

I could feel the voice penetrating my being, infecting my brain, making me feel tired. Then I felt flushed with a sense of evil and hate and ugliness. My nostrils flared, reacting to a sudden, awful stench. Visions of death and decay flooded into my mind. I felt myself being torn within, as if two teams were playing a deadly game of tug-of-war with my soul.

The deep, resonant voice of God returned.

"I have chosen you," He began repeating.

But the new voice, the syrupy whine, is insistent, more intense now, higher in pitch.

"Come with me," it demands, and then again, almost screeching.

I could feel the evil presence come against me. My skin crawled with a repulsive clamminess. I felt smothered and sick. The presence—whatever it was—was trying to enter me, to penetrate my being. The voice became more vile, more desperate, taunting me.

And I knew I was being harassed by Satan himself —a being I had never believed existed. I knew now that I was wrestling with the devil.

My mind was boggled. Satan had been a myth, make-believe. He had been just another ghost story on a dark and stormy night, the stuff Hollywood makes horror movies of.

Now, in the trauma of the moment, I knew I'd been wrong. I was being molested by Satan. It was really happening.

The anguish boiled up in my throat.

"God! Help me!" I cried out.

Briefly, I was alone again. Satan, I could sense, was a short distance away—having fled before the name of God, but only for a moment.

I caught my breath and tried to get a grip on my reeling mind, but there was no rest. Suddenly I was filled with an intense dread—all of the internal alarms went off inside me. Like the driver whose doom becomes evident in the split-second before the crash, I knew I was going to die.

I'm going to die! I screamed silently inside my head, with absolute, unrestrained horror.

The moment lasted forever. Death hung heavy over my head. I saw myself in a morgue with other bodies. I saw my family crying over my grave.

<u>I'm going to die! I'm going to die right now!</u>

"I have chosen you," the reassuring voice responded. "You are not going to die." His was a booming voice, and yet clear, authoritative but gentle. Instantly the images of death vanished, and the panic subsided into peacefulness.

Once again my courage picked up. I felt reassured. I felt God's friendship, His kinship. I felt warm and comforted.

But I heard a laugh, a sniggering laugh from somewhere in the darkness. A slippery, slimy sensation enveloped my senses. Images appeared before my eyes, as if projected on a giant screen.

I was seeing myself. All of those times in my life when I had done something wrong were being shown back to me. As I watched, I was embarrassed, then ashamed. When the long chronicle was over, I began to watch scenes of the things I had only wished for—worse things than what I had actually done! I watched myself participating in sin after sin after sin—a repulsive but exciting but disgusting but exhilarating experience. My emotions became tangled and knotted.

A lovely feminine voice began to whisper enticing temptations into my ear. I knew I had to resist, but my insides were drawn, drawn, drawn. My emotions were screaming for pleasure, longing for fulfillment. My intellect was desperately holding the line.

"No!" I finally shouted, almost helplessly. "I won't give in."

And again, darkness. I peered into it, looking for

something, anything. I strained to hear something, anything.

There was a low murmuring all around me, as if I were in the midst of a huge group of grumbling people. Before me, suddenly, stood a huge black door. The air began to glow and shimmer with oppressive heat.

I watched as the door opened upon a vast, flaming oven. I felt myself drawn like a magnet into the center of the flames–although I was terrified to go in. There were hundreds of others already there, roasting to death, but not dead. Once I was inside, the door slammed shut behind me. The worst, dreadest feelings sloshed around inside me, like so much poison.

"Is this actually what hell is?" I asked aloud.

I passed my hands through blue-tipped flames. The fire itself was cold, and it did not hurt me. From nowhere, a thought flashed through my mind: <u>Death, where is thy sting?</u> Satan's sting, I realized–somehow –had been dulled. God, even in the midst of this holocaust, was truly in control of everything. I began to laugh, and the others laughed with me, at Satan's futility. Our laughter bounced off the walls of the oven and echoed over the roar of the flames.

And instantly, as if someone had flipped the channel selector, I was alone again in darkness.

I sighed, weary. I could not regulate my feelings, and now I was feeling abandoned and lonely. I longed to be with my family. I wanted to tell them how much I loved them. I needed to tell everyone how much God loved them!

"You will tell others about me, Don" the voice of God said, out of nowhere. "That is your mission. That is why you are going through these experiences."

I listened patiently.

"You must learn to love others, to have compassion and to forgive them. You must live that others may see me in you."

In a flash, I could recall every person I had ever held a grudge against, every quarrel I had ever left unresolved. In the dog-eat-dog world of television advertising, there were dozens.

Instantly I found myself back in the hospital bed, with Mary sitting beside me.

"Mary?" I said softly, discovering that my body was surprisingly weak.

"Yes, Don," she responded kindly. "What is it?"

"I want you to call some people for me," I said to her. "I want you to tell them that I love them and that God cares about them. This is very important, Mary."

Mary dutifully got out a pen and piece of paper, and proceeded to write down names as I reeled them off. There were friends, business associates, other acquaintances. Faithfully, without questioning me, Mary headed for a pay phone.

I did not realize it then, but I had just begun my ministry.

6.

Take This Job and Shove It

I T never occurred to Mary Brubaker not to believe her husband's story. As he began to unfold the events he was experiencing in another world–in brief periods of conversation, between long, sedated hours of sleep–she accepted every word. The look in his tired eyes, the tone in his voice, even weak as his voice had become–the look and the tone told her he was telling her the absolute truth.

She did not understand it all, but she did not feel she had to. She believed.

Terrie believed her father from the first moment she heard him tell any of it. Something about the way he talked convinced her–even though much of what he was saying was contrary to what she had come to believe about hell, Satan, and the existence of evil.

Cindy, always believed her father. It had always been her nature to be open, receptive, and especially to her dad. He had never told her anything that turned out to be untrue. So now, even for all the strangeness of her father's stories, Cindy had no trouble accepting every word. But as to the meaning of it all–Cindy didn't have a clue.

Young Jeff, frightened and angered by the cataclysm that had invaded his life in the form of his father's heart attack, had other things to think about. The truth or madness of his father's tales did not concern him much at the moment.

Jeff's life was soon to take a nasty turn.

It was the hospital staff who reacted with the most anxiety to Don's stories about the other realm of existence. They were medical professionals, clinical in their outlook on life. Don Brubaker's self-described meanderings through an unseen dimension by and large did not set well with their scientific viewpoint. And yet, many listened, and came back to listen some more. When his strength allowed it, Don was an engaging conversationalist, with a warm sense of humor –a favored patient in an institution full of people unhappy about being there. And, because of his precarious medical condition, Don's stay stretched beyond days into weeks, and then beyond weeks into months. So he became a regular citizen of the place, known to all.

But his stories got mixed reviews. Some felt he was having a one-in-a-million reaction to the drugs, although this theory was almost unsettling scientifically as the stories themselves. Others felt his subconscious was reacting to the stress of living so close to the edge of death. And yet, who could deny that he was able to recall minute details of events going on around him—even while all the medical personnel could confirm that he was completely unconscious?

Eerily, each new coronary arrest, each new brush with death, brought a new story, a new series of experiences. Afterward, with another medical crisis behind them, the nurses on the floor began to hear from Don—in bits and pieces, as his strength allowed—what had happened during those frenetic moments while they struggled to keep his body alive. And, each time, he could tell them what had happened to him, somewhere else, as well as what had happened to them—in the hospital room.

For nurse Debbie, the whole affair was a wearing one. She had come to Osteopathic Hospital as a fresh, open-hearted novice. After a couple of months on the periphery of Don Brubaker, she felt like a ruddy veteran. Don's stories made her nervous. She knew he was not hallucinating. She knew it medically—she had seen patients hallucinating, and she had seen the accompanying effects: many forgot their hallucinations afterward, or, if they remembered them, they dismissed them as the mental illusions they really were. But Don did not forget, and did not dismiss, what he had seen. Moreover, she could tell that Don was actually <u>living</u> the experiences he was describing.

And the subject matter spooked her. Hell, Satan, eternity. It all made her wonder what the future held for her. It was not pleasant stuff to fill the midnight shift.

Veteran Bertha could not help but connect her first husband's deathbed experience to Don's. She was convinced they had experienced similar phenomena, although Don's was even more profound and real. When she told some of the other nurses what she thought, they laughed at her. But Bertha didn't change her mind.

One evening, toward the end of her shift, Don jolted into a crisis. As people came running from all corners, Don called out. Bertha was closest, and responded.

"Hold my hand," Don cried, his face full of fear, "so the devil can't take me!"

Bertha clutched his hand and peered into the patient's face. This, she knew, was no hallucination. This man was facing something more awful than she had ever experienced.

As Don's stay dragged on, Bertha watched the scene again and again. Not only was Don struggling for his life; he was struggling for his soul. Bertha could not be sure that the doctors were doing the right thing by going to such extremes to bring this man back from literal death—at least not so often. She felt there was something supernatural at work here, and she couldn't be sure what it was. Or why.

The day came when Don's monitor began beeping and Bertha did not come running. She grabbed a clipboard and chart instead, and designated herself bookkeeper for the event. Someone always had to record such episodes for the file—she decided to do it herself, rather than help the doctors play God.

The crises kept coming, day after day, week after week. Bertha began to wear down. She had been at this nursing stuff for a long, long time anyway. Now she was wishing she could spend more time with her family, and be more involved in her church. . . .

One Sunday morning proved the turning point. She had just come in from the night shift. She was beat. Her husband wanted her to get ready for church, but she was too tired. They argued briefly. Suddenly Bertha blurted, "I just wish I could quit!"

Her husband looked at her sternly. "Do whatever you have to do," he said. And he left with the children for church.

Bertha returned to the hospital and resigned her position, burned out. She had cared for Don Brubaker for more than three months. It had pushed her over the edge.

Bertha took a part-time job in a laundromat.

* * *

Lynn observed that Don Brubaker was getting to some of the nurses. Some, in fact, were literally afraid to work with him. His delicate condition required constant monitoring, and everyone knew that any one of them, with only the slightest miscalculation, could kill him in an instant. Besides, his unusual experiences—all that out-of-the-body stuff—were frightening.

But Lynn, unafraid, took a special interest in Don. She was not a particularly religious person, but in lis-

tening to Don relate his experiences, she was convinced
that there was a force out there, somewhere, that was
stronger and bigger than man. She wasn't sure about
there being a God, Old Testament style, but Don might
make a believer out of her yet, she figured.

Lynn saw the fear in the staff and understood it.
She also saw the fear in Don—and that, she knew, was
reasonable too. Don's condition was perhaps as critical
as it could get for a living person. Examinations revealed that Don had been born with unusually small
arteries—a genetic deficiency—on the right side of his
heart. As a result of this, the right ventricle of the heart
was constantly starved for blood. The heart attack,
fiendishly, had damaged the good portion. The left side
of his heart now suffered from a severe aneurism—a
killer "bubble" that could explode without warning. The
two halves of the heart, engineered to work together,
were now fighting each other for survival—and threatening to destroy the very life of Don Brubaker in the
process. Medical people had a nickname for Don's kind
of condition: they called it the widow-maker.

Because of the huge dosages of medication he was
on, Don's blood pressure was very low. Lynn could never
quite get used to his pale, pasty complexion. And almost by the day, she could see his weight shrinking,
pound after pound after pound, until his flesh hung
limp on his bones.

But Lynn's job was survival, and she determined to
give Don Brubaker the fightingest chance he could pos-
sibly have. The day would come, she figured, when he

would leave the hospital, if only to die at home—and he would need to know how to take care of himself. Quite literally, he would need to know how not to kill himself.

Over the next weeks and months, Lynn began to educate Don, to train him in survival skills. She eased him into the full realization of the kind of life he would have to lead—giving up a lot of what he had once considered normal, taking life very easy, living almost like a house pet, with no mandated activity, no rigid agenda of accomplishments. She taught him some simple exercises that he could do to gradually build his strength back up.

Still, she knew the doctors didn't give him more than six months to live once he left the womb of the hospital. And she couldn't make a more hopeful prediction herself. Medically speaking, Don Brubaker was doomed. A widow-maker.

7.

Trip Number Three

DON hears his monitor sounding off, and he can feel his heart pumping wildly. Suddenly, almost expectantly, he is thrust into the cold darkness. Still, he is watching the activity in his room at the same time.

In the tunnel, he is being assaulted by Satan again. The devil is offering all sorts of wonderful enticements. And Don can hear the voice of God reaffirming that he has been chosen.

The torment and struggle continue for what seem like hours. He again feels the tug-of-war. He feels as if he can't take it much longer, he needs to rest, to regain his strength. If only he could get away from this torment for a moment!

A thought streaks into his embattled mind: <u>Let yourself into the blue!</u> Reacting on instinct alone, Don asks out loud to be in the blue.

Suddenly he is enveloped and floating in a deep, electric blue sky. It is the most amazing and beautiful blue he has ever seen. It feels velvety soft. The air seems to sparkling with purity. He is at peace, feeling restful, serene.

Don perceives a light moving toward him. It is bluish white and giving off small yellow flashes and sparks at the edges, growing in intensity until it is almost too intense to look into.

And there is a figure in the middle of the light. Don's very being leaps in recognition that this is Jesus Christ. It's Christ coming toward him. Don gazes at His extraordinarily handsome face. The eyes are full of love and acceptance. Don is immersed in a feeling of joy and hope and all good things.

Christ's voice rings gently, like the sound of tiny, pleasant silver bells.

"Don, do you want to stay here, or do you wish to go back?"

Don hesitates to answer. He is wrapped in a warm sense of love and peace. The color is such a pleasure to see and feel. And Jesus indicates no impatience.

Don realizes that he is grinning like a little boy getting his first puppy.

I am seeing God's own Son. This is the Lord. This is Jesus!

Suddenly, a soft sense of sadness creeps into Don's thoughts. He thinks of his dear family. He can sense the sorrow they would feel if he were gone. Don knows he must go back to them, that he has work to do.

Don wonders about that. It was God who gave him his mission. Why, then, if God wants him to minister to others, is Jesus offering him an opportunity to stay here in heaven?

The answer surfaces from his own thoughts. This is a test. Again, Christ speaks: "Don, do you want to stay or go back?"

"I want to go back," Don answers immediately, knowing he has made the right choice.

Jesus smiles.

"You have chosen well. Go. I am with you," Jesus says gently.

Immediately Don is back in his hospital bed. But the light–and Christ's presence–are still very real to him. He hears Christ's voice speaking softly in his mind.

"Your physical healing will take a long time, but you will live. Remember that. You will recall all of your experiences clearly, and you will write a book. You must tell others about me and about Satan. You must make them understand that there are very real choices they must make. I have chosen you for this work. You will succeed. You will be safe. I am always nearby. You are never alone."

Don falls asleep. When he awakes, a deep-seated fear of the unknown crawls into his mind. Again, the thought that he is going to die grips him. He's sure he will die tonight. A voice hisses in his ear.

"Don, you are going to die. If you don't believe me, feel the bed move beneath you. Look at the people standing beside you. Ask them if you're going to die!"

Terror presses into Don's subconscious. A group of gray-faced, dark-robed people surround his bed.

"Am I going to die!" Don pleads.

They all nod their heads, and the bed even moves up and down, solemnly, in affirmation.

Don is convinced they are right. He must take action.

"Debbie!" he calls out to the night nurse. "I've got to make my will!"

Debbie, terrified, tries to calm her harried patient. But Don will not be calmed. With the gray, morbid troupe still standing over him, he repeats his instructions to her over and over, until she convinces him that she understands. Finally, he releases her, and she hurries away.

Sick with worry, Don reaches out to touch the flesh of one of the gray people standing around his bed, hoping somehow to discover that they are not real. But he can feel the flesh, clammy and spongy, as if it has been dragged through a swamp.

Don feels lost, forsaken. God promised he would live, yet these creatures are affirming that he will die. And they are real. It isn't a dream. Don reasons that he must have misunderstood God's intentions.

Gently, firmly, the voice of God echoes once again in Don's mind. "I have chosen you," He says. "You will live. The devil is a liar, and so are his servants. You will live."

Relief flows once again through Don's being. The gray presences, thus challenged, dissipate like ghosts. Now Don sees clearly: he was being harassed by Satan again. But God—as always—was in control.

A nurse hurries into the room. She is smiling as she approaches Don's bed in quick steps.

"Don, I'm going to have to hit you on the chest," she says, but with reassuring authority in her voice.

She chops him squarely in the chest. Don sees the blow coming and expects to be rocked by it. But he is surprised to find that he doesn't feel a thing. Suddenly he realizes he is watching the scene like a movie, from above. He feels no pain, although he knows he should.

There are more thumps, but they don't work. Doctors come running to administer shock. Don can feel his body being charged with huge bangs of electricity, but there is still no pain. He watches and listens as they work to revive his floundering heart.

And then, slowly, darkness creeps in around him. He watches the hospital room recede, like a TV picture shrinking into a tiny dot in the center. There is nothing left but a small blip of light, then total darkness. He is in the tunnel again.

The red eye is staring intently at him. Together they are traveling very fast through the tunnel—and then a maze of many tunnels, with tight, twisting curves.

Don's senses seem to be more acute than ever before. He can see, feel, and hear more this time. Details are clearer. The wind is whipping past his face, blowing his hair. He's not cold, even though he is only wearing a flimsy hospital gown.

The red eye's gaze seems to pierce Don's very being.

They have slowed down, and Don can hear a mumbling voice coming from an adjacent tunnel. Immediately he and the red eye moved toward the sound. Don knows he is out of control. The red eye is in charge now.

He is practically thrust into this new, murky tunnel. The mumbling is growing louder. Don is floating now, near the top of a long cavernous passageway. Below him, he can barely make out several forms, some kind of hairy creatures. They are moving through the muddy tunnel, and as they walk, their feet are making slurping, sticking sounds that mix with their mumbling to fill the tunnel with a sad sound: "Mug-wump, mug-wump, mug-wump . . ."

The light becomes a little clearer, and Don sees that these are people. They have very long, dirty hair that reaches down to their toes. It is matted with wet clay-like mud. Some of them, though it's hard to see, seem to be carrying—yes, they are—Bibles under their arms!

Don floats slowly above them, unable to understand who or what these creatures are—except that it seems natural to call them "mug-wumps." Strangely, he feels an affinity toward them.

Slowly Don begins to perceive their faces. He recognizes some of them—they are friends of his! He can't remember their names, but he knows them. He suddenly feels a great compassion toward all these muddy, pathetic beings. His heart seems to leap out toward them.

Gradually, the pieces come together in Don's mind. These people were once part-time believers, Sunday-only Christians, doubters. The are fence-riders, with their mugs on one side and their wumps on the other!

Don and the mugwumps move down the passageway, Don in the air above them. The walls are covered

with a slimy ooze. The tunnel begins to twist and turn
sharply and grow smaller, winding downwards. Don
fears he's in for some navigating problems. The mugwumps below him are moving in a single file now; there
isn't enough room for them to move two or more abreast.
The turns become sharper, and Don can tell he's not
going to make it through. He's going to get stuck in
this mess. He feels himself beginning to choke with
panic.

Desperately, he tells himself this isn't real. It must
be a dream! he says, striving to convince himself. He
tries to wake up, to wish himself away, out of the tunnel—but to no avail. The air is becoming even staler
and thinner. Don feels smothered.

The turn up ahead is particularly sharp. Don shiv-
ers. He can't make the turn. He's going to get stuck.

No. Don's eyes grow wide as he watches his body
dissolve through the stone, as if the rock were air. His
mind reels as he and the mugwumps continue down on
their forlorn trek. What is happening to me?

The tunnel seems endless. Don realizes somehow
that these creatures have been in the tunnel for a very
long time. Something tells him that they could leave if
they wanted—if only they would look up. Still, it's easier
not to. It's easier just to follow along with the others,
trapped between doubt and faith.

Then the passage widens dramatically, and Don can
breathe again. As they turn the corner, Don can see
light ahead—brilliant light, light that floods the end of
the tunnel as they approach.

There, at the end, is a large iron gate. On the other side of the gate is a beautiful meadow. The sun is shining brightly and the grass is a rich emerald green. Don can even hear a multitude of birds singing cheerily.

The mugwumps, though, are unmoved by the scene. They continue milling around in the cave, mumbling. It's obvious to Don that they could leave this dull, morose place if they wanted—they could be out in that meadow. They could move from doubt to clarity of faith. Yet, they resist. They doubt the meadow is real. They doubt that God can truly forgive them. They cling to their Bibles but never read them. They're stuck in this Inferno-like limbo.

Don longs for the meadow, longs to be away from these creatures. And the moment he thinks it, he passes through the gate—just as he had passed through the stone. The gate, he realizes, is the illusion—not the meadow! The mugwumps have created the illusion of the gate to deny the reality they refuse to accept.

What a tragedy! Don says to himself as he walks through the meadow, enjoying the clean air and the sweet fragrance of flowers and trees. The colors are indescribable. Everything pulses with a rich, sensual intensity. The air is filled with a kind of music, a music made by the meadow. It's a pleasant and calming chord. Don feels that old feeling once again: I could stay here forever!

Then, instantly, Don finds himself retreating back through the tunnel above the obnoxious mugwumps. He moves rapidly and returns to his hospital bed in only a matter of seconds. Still in the presence of the mugwumps, he sees a nurse entering the room. Don tries to explain to her what is happening to him. She looks nervously at his chart and assures him that the drugs he has had are not hallucinatory. Perhaps, she says, he is just dreaming. Don knows better.

Everything changes again, as if someone has turned a page in a book. Don sees himself in the midst of a huge crowd. It's not a modern crowd. They are dressed in the clothes of Bible times. He looks down at himself. So is he!

The crowd seems to be jeering at Don. Why? he wonders. Then he sees more: he is helping a man, someone who has been brutally whipped and abused. The crowd is upset because Don is offering assistance. But the beaten man has eyes that burn with love and compassion.

How could anyone want to hurt this man? Don wonders. He lifts the man off of the dusty road to his feet.

The man turns, and from somewhere he lifts a huge wooden cross to his back. The man begins moving toward a hill. The hill is called Golgotha. With each new moment, Don realizes more and more clearly what he is seeing.

These people are going to crucify Christ.

Don follows, stunned. He watches in horror as Jesus is nailed to the cross, the spikes pounded through His wrists and the sensitive insteps of his feet. He watches helpless as the cross is propped up and dropped into position with an ugly thud. Don covers his face with his hands.

If only others could see what I've seen, he says to himself, grief-stricken. The world would get on its knees. . . . The world would be at peace!

Don opens his eyes. He is in the hospital bed, Mary at his side, telling him to rest. Stop talking and rest, she says—but Don wants to talk. He wants to tell everybody. Has she heard what he just said? She assures him she had—but stop talking and rest.

Don's thoughts shroud him, and soon he is asleep.

How can I stop talking and rest? There is so much work to do!

8.

Tunnel Vision

Y rest period was very brief. No sooner had I settled back than I began to feel very peculiar. When I closed my eyes, suddenly I could see Jesus on the cross, the mugwumps, the tunnel, and the red eye—everything at once! And when I opened my eyes, I could still see all these things, but I could also see the hospital room and Mary at my side as well.

What a fantastic sensation, I said to myself. I could see, hear, feel, taste, and smell things from both worlds simultaneously.

For some unexplainable reason, then, a foolish fear popped into my mind. I felt that if I closed my eyes too long, I would be lost to the other reality forever. I began telling Mary about it, expressing my fear. But Mary, as always, was quick to encourage me, unshakable in her faith.

"Don't worry, Don. God promised to take care of you. You won't leave us. Relax. Many people are praying for you all over the country."

I drew strength from Mary's presence. I knew then I would be all right. The terror dissipated as she spoke.

I knew that there was more I must learn about what had happened to me. It would take time, I realized, to sort out all of my experiences and thoughts. I felt compelled to start putting some of this on paper as soon as possible. <u>I must record everything accurately and report to others all I have seen and heard</u>, I determined inwardly.

I understood that my body and soul were being put to the test, and that I would survive. I regretted that I had never really studied the Bible. I knew now—much too late—that it would have helped me in this situation. Or, indeed, made the situation unnecessary entirely!

I had read bits and pieces of the Bible when I was in Sunday school years before. I had learned a few of the select passages, mostly in little contests between the students. I had done well; I won my share of trinket-prizes.

But I hadn't really studied.

I could remember praying with my mother at bedtime. I would call out to God periodically when things had gotten rough and I needed help. But I had never in any way committed my life to the Lord. If anybody had suggested, I would have considered it a silly idea.

Such a commitment was unnecessary in the world of Self.

But now, every Bible passage that I could recall suddenly became important, as I floated in this strange netherworld. They were like life preservers, buoying me up. I reached deep into my mind for whatever shreds I could recall. Mary read some Scriptures to me almost every day, and each word seemed to sink into my subconscious, as if I were a dry sponge, longing for life.

* * *

In the other place, I suddenly began falling backwards and sideways at the same time. I was moving so rapidly that I felt faint. The air became heavy and musty. Again I was in the tunnel, with the evil red eye glaring at me.

Fear fed into my groping mind. The air rushing past me was cold, clammy. Terror was clawing at my insides, as if something alien possessed me. The dread that held me was like being in a speeding car without brakes.

A hideous presence suddenly filled the tunnel. I stopped. I was short of breath and felt pressure. I was being squeezed by the rocks around me. I was trapped in the stone walls. My worst fear was coming true. I was going to be entombed in those filthy cave walls! I felt colder still, and more exhausted.

The whining voice began to taunt me again. It was asking me why I should continue going through this agony. It told me I could be healed and made wealthy if I would give in to him.

"Ask for anything," he said sensuously, "and it can be yours. Anything!"

Visions of wealth appeared before my eyes, like a three-dimensional movie. Diamonds, money, cars, gold, beautiful women, everything. I was overwhelmed by the vision. I could almost touch it, it seemed so real.

I realized, though, that I was merely being toyed with again. It was all the devil's illusion. <u>But it would be so easy to give in!</u> I told myself. Still, I resisted, wondering how in the world I was doing it, wondering where I was getting the strength to resist.

Satan persisted in his bargaining for my soul. I struggled to clear my mind of the images and the lust. In one ear, I heard the words <u>Enjoy, enjoy.</u> In the other, I heard <u>Resist, resist.</u>

I wanted it to end. I had seen Christ. I <u>knew</u> what I was choosing! The devil be damned!

Thoughts and phrases of peace flooded my mind. "Jesus lives in you," I heard. "God has promised you life." Instantly I found myself back in the beautiful meadow, out of the evil presence. I rested in the garden.

* * *

I felt as if I had no will of my own, that all of this had been planned for me. It was like being on a sort of guided tour.

I felt alert, and knew that I was very ill physically. I understood that I had suffered a serious heart attack, with complications. I was even aware of everything that the doctors and nurses had talked about, how my body was responding to their treatments.

I knew I had been talking to Mary and the children, all of whom had spent more hours around my hospital bed than I could even begin to imagine, but I couldn't remember everything I had told them. Still, they all seemed to understand that I was going through some kind of odd ordeal. And they knew I was going to write a book. They knew of the places I had been, and that I had spoken with God, and with Jesus Christ.

I didn't know how many of the people I had talked to believed me—nurses, doctors, friends. But even the doubters had no rational explanation for what was happening.

* * *

As I opened my eyes, I knew I was in my hospital bed. I felt a very reassuring touch and saw a young man in a white uniform. My mind was working very slowly. For some reason, I felt a great sense of trust toward this young man. He was a nurse, and he was talking to me.

The nurse seemed to know that I had been "out of body." He was puzzled by my experiences, but not surprised. He talked with me about my experiences with a fair amount of knowledge. I learned that the young man was a Christian. He and I became good friends over the next few weeks.

Mary came into the room. I had called for her earlier. I had felt compelled to tell her of my latest experiences.

As I talked with her, I sensed a difference inside myself. I felt cleaner and new. The thought repeated itself over and over in my mind: <u>I must be born again! I am born again!</u>

Suddenly I shouted out loud: "I've been born again!"

Mary tried to quiet me. "Don't get so worked up, honey," she said firmly. "You'll jerk your tubes out. You've been working too hard. You need to rest."

Mary pointed out that even God rested on the seventh day. So should I, she added.

Seven days? It was my first awareness of time. I had been in the hospital for a full week. It seemed like only a day! But how had I been there so long without going to the bathroom, without eating? Suddenly I was very concerned, and when I asked Mary about it I must have sounded frantic.

Mary reassured me: I had eaten. And everything else, she added prudently, had been taken care of to. I just didn't remember.

"Why is everything else so clear in my mind," I wondered, "but I can't even remember going to the bathroom?"

It was at that moment that the full realization hit me. My experiences were real. They were not dreams or hallucinations. I had really lived "out of body" in another dimension, off and on for the past week.

I felt extremely tired at the thought of it. I must have really been working hard, as Mary had said. I felt if I could sleep—really sleep, without traveling around—I might get well sooner.

"You have been healed, in the spirit," I heard a silent voice whisper in my mind. "Now you must trust in your doctors for your body's healing. You will be totally well."

My voice, I noticed, didn't sound right. I seemed hoarse. Mary told me I was hoarse because I had been talking continually all week. Often I had shouted and created quite a disturbance. But I never knew it.

All at once, I saw Mary hurrying away, and a nurse rushed into the room.

"Don, I'm going to have to hit you on the chest again."

I felt almost foolish.

"Okay, get it over with," I responded.

I watched her fist hitting my chest. I felt nothing. No pain. But I could feel the air being pushed out of my lungs by the blows. The nurse smiled. "Okay, you've been converted," she said, satisfied with her work.

"I know I've been converted," I replied, smiling. "I've been born again!"

The nurse blushed a bit and explained that she meant the term in the medical sense. My heart, she said, had slowed to a normal rate again.

We laughed together at the misunderstanding.

"You must be getting better," she said. "Your sense of humor is picking up."

Still, time passed in swirls. It was difficult for me to keep one day, one hour, separate from the next. My only reference points were the nurses' shift changes.

9.

Angels and the Light

DON had grown accustomed to all of the monitors and machinery that surrounded his bed and were attached to his body. The I-Vac ticked softly like a clock, doling out just the right amount of medication through Don's IV tube and into his veins. It became a comforting sound.

He could also see his heart monitor with the blipping line. The irregular line bothered him at first, until a nurse explained that this was the way it was supposed to be. She said a squiggly line was better than no line at all! And Don agreed.

Don's world in the hospital room was small and orderly. This was important to him. It gave him a sense of stability. It was his reference point. Many serious heart attack patients experience the same need for order and security.

One night, one of the nurses removed the I-Vac while Don was asleep. The silence woke him. His stomach flopped when he found the machine gone.

"There's a shortage of machines," she explained, "and we can regulate your medicine manually. A little child needs the machine more than you do."

Don still wasn't comfortable without the machine. He felt sorry for the child, but also for himself. He had become very dependent on the presence of the machine. Finally, after some gentle prodding by Don, the nurse located another and brought it in. As it began ticking away once again, Don sighed and slouched back into his pillow.

* * *

In the morning, all Don could see out his window was snow. Everything was covered with white fluff. A radio announcer announced jauntily that this was the worst winter Michigan had ever experienced.

Don could see the tall pine trees bowed by the heavy load of snow. Big black crows were flying in search of food and shelter. He felt encouraged by the life he saw outside.

Then he squinted. His vision, he noticed, was funny. Distances and close-up objects were clear. But the middle distances were fuzzy. Don felt a wad of tension growing in his gut. It was just a common reaction to some of his medication, a nurse insisted. But the explanation didn't help him much.

The weight of dependency began to take its toll on Don Brubaker. As he began to stabilize medically after the first week in the hospital, his medication was gradually diminished in quantity, and his periods of wakefulness grew longer—and more disquieting. He began to realize how helpless he was, and helplessness did not agree with him. He had always done for himself in everything. Now he had to learn to trust others for even his simplest needs. It was disconcerting—and humbling. A healthy thing, but hard.

Mary moved into town, with friends. Bob's family lived close to the hospital, which made their kind offer too convenient to pass by. Mary made a point of assuring Don that all their financial needs were being taken care of, that he shouldn't worry about a thing. And Jeff, the only child still living at home stayed out in the country with other friends, so he could stay in school there. As often as the lousy weather would permit, Jeff could come and visit his dad.

Don felt like all the bases had been covered adequately.

What a wonderful family, Don said to himself. His affection for them welled up inside, more than ever before. But there's a new element to his love for them now—a definite difference that he can sense, very specifically, almost tangibly: he is anxious to lead them to Christ, to help them experience the fullness of that love that he had experienced himself, face to face with the Son of God.

It was a longing to love them more than he had, to love them in a new way, a way that he had never known. Finally, Don had learned the value of love. And he wanted to express it! It was, he realized now, the most important thing in life. His old attitude seemed silly to him, all of a sudden. Now, he couldn't wait to be up and hugging everyone in sight, telling everyone that they were <u>loved</u>!

Cards and letters arrived daily from friends and relatives. Everyone assured him of their prayers. Don drew strength from the messages, and basked in the love and concern others were showing for him. He was learning daily to appreciate his friends—something he had never taken time to do before.

It was a time of wonder for Don Brubaker. He was filled with awe by his own thoughts, of his reactions to his adventures. One moment, scared stiff. The next, completely and perfectly at peace.

* * *

Still innocent in the faith, Don had not yet made much of a distinction between various faiths. The group steeped in mysticism, was as acceptable to him as the Reformed Church in Traverse City. The pastor from there had been asked to visit Don, by one of the pastor's neighbors, Tim, who was Don's sales manager. The pastor and the patient immediately took to each other, and they visited frequently, developing a solid friendship with Don and Mary.

But the pastor's scriptural input didn't completely replace the reservoir of mysticism that Don had stored up within himself. So, when the people from the group decided to have a special prayer session on behalf of Don one Wednesday evening at nine, Don was only too happy to join in with them in meditation at the same time. Together in thought, their energies would unite —and the healing process, Don figured ignorantly, would hasten.

By the time Mary had left his room (heading for the C.C.U. family room, where she would be meditating at the appointed hour, too), Don felt tired. But it was almost nine, and time to align himself with the people's thoughts.

Abruptly, a light entered the room. Don was startled. For the first time in many days, he was not traveling out of his body. He looked around, nonplussed. He was still very much in the hospital room—and nowhere else.

The light surrounded his bed like a large halo. Then, suddenly, six beings appeared around his bed—tall people, beautiful people, with dark olive skin, dressed in long white robes, with penetrating blue eyes. Each of them was very solemn and intent.

The light began to pulsate, and became like a single shaft of sunlight. First it shone on Don's face, then it moved over his body, slowly, deliberately, almost as if it were searching for something.

Wherever it touched, Don could feel a comforting warmth. He closed his eyes, just to enjoy the feeling of the light.

119

When he opened his eyes, the six were still there. No one spoke a word, but Don could feel their love, their caring. Don tried to speak, but found that he couldn't. He wanted to ask questions, to discover who these beings were, but his mouth would not open. He felt as if he had been struck dumb.

Don wondered momentarily if he were having a genuine, old-fashioned dream. He reached over and rang for the nurse.

"What's wrong?" she asked as she entered.

"Do you see the men around my bed?" Don asked.

The nurse could not conceal the look that came across her face. She humored her patient for a few moments, holding his hand—and then left.

But Don's six angels were still very much at work.

The light narrowed, until finally it had become nearly a pinpoint. It moved across his chest, making small circling motions. Then it moved down his stomach, down his legs, then back and down his arms. Don felt warm all over. And everywhere the light touched, he felt comfort.

Suddenly he realized that a seventh person had appeared. He was smaller than the others, standing at the foot of the bed. Dressed in a dark three-piece suit, he had a black goatee. It occurred to Don that the man could be an Egyptian businessman. But there was something chilling about this figure, something unpleasant.

The six ignored him.

As he stared at Don, he spoke, but not to Don.

"You're working too hard, Olivia."

Don blinked, surprised. Olivia was the name of the person leading the meditation group at that very moment. Don stared back into the man's face, trying to place him. Maybe Mary would know. Don studied the man, to remember every detail. He wanted to be able to describe him in detail to Mary–to make whatever connection with Olivia there was to be made.

Then, without warning, the man disappeared. The heat of the angels' light dropped in intensity. The six were still standing in silent vigil around the bed. The light became wider, more like a flood lamp, bathing Don's upper chest in warm, moist heat. Don was unworried. The warm light was still comforting.

He couldn't tell how long it lasted. He noticed the snow falling outside the window, as the figures stood silent. Then he fell asleep.

* * *

When Don awoke, very early in the morning, no one was in the room. His body, however, still felt warm.

He tried to explain the experience to the morning nurse. She dismissed it: a dream, she said. But when Mary came in, as he expected, she believed him fully. And she recognized Don's description of the small man in the three-piece suit: it was Omar, Olivia's guru.

Mary hurried to a pay phone and called Olivia. She was excited that the group had made such tangible contact with Don–but she was concerned about the

121

heat. After Mary described the entire incident, Olivia agreed: they had been working too hard, generating too much healing light.

Olivia's lie fell far short of expressing the danger that Don had unknowingly faced. It would be months before Don and Mary understood that God had sent His angels to protect Don from the onslaught of the enemy.

And Omar, one of Satan's own, had visited the room to find out what was obstructing the group's prayers.

* * *

Don had always thought of himself as a rational, level-headed person. Now, as he thought back over his experiences of the past few weeks, his head throbbed. All of this stuff was taxing to his powers of logic. Nothing in his life could have prepared him for what he had gone through.

He could feel frustration welling up inside. On one hand, he was fully convinced that he would get well and leave the hospital room. But on the other hand, he was still haunted by thoughts of death—and that feeling of uncertainty, a certainty that he was going to die.

The doctors and nurses were all reassuring him that he was coming along as well as could be expected. Mary assured him too, reminding him that God had promised to make him well.

All of which helped. Except that, whenever he was left alone, fear crept back into his mind.

Don could not know that he was caught in the midst of spiritual warfare, that the spirit world was at work on his psyche, fighting for his mind, struggling to short-circuit his God-given mission.

Don could tell, as he strove to still his troubled thoughts, that he needed to turn to prayer. It was the only thing that could calm his doubts—he was convinced of that. But prayer was something new for him. He had never really prayed, ever, except for the little memorized ditties of childhood.

Awkwardly, oddly, Don felt his way, doing the best he could. As it turned out, he simply talked to God. But somehow it felt all right—and Don felt he was beginning to understand what it meant to have a personal relationship with the Lord.

* * *

Off in the distance Don could hear a rumble. One of the nurses rushed into the room. Don knew what was happening before she even spoke.

"Don, I'm going to . . ."

Don watched as her fist struck him solidly on the sternum, the slightly curved bone in the middle of the chest. He felt no pain, as usual. She hit him again, then a third time. She looked concerned and turned to press a red button on the wall.

The call for "Dr. Hart" crackled over the hospital intercom. The monitor alarm began to sound.

Don was surrounded in a matter of moments by

white-clothed doctors and nurses. One nurse prepared a huge needle. Others prepared the paddles. As they applied the shock, Don's body nearly jumped off the bed. Still, he could feel no pain.

Don suddenly felt himself tumbling backwards, out of the bed. He watched as the room distorted and began to fade into the distance. He felt a single, sharp pain, then everything was suddenly cold and dark. He was in the tunnel again.

A roar, like a speeding train, boomed through the tunnel, and Don could see the red eye coming at him. The wind was tearing past him as he and the eye sped through the dank tunnel. He felt as if the bottom of his stomach had fallen out.

Don could feel evil emanating from the red eye.

Suddenly, Don felt the immense pressure of a sudden, desperate stop, and he felt himself crash into the floor of the tunnel. His breath was knocked out of him. He gasped for air. Far away, at the end of the tunnel, a light flickered. Then it twinkled, then it vanished.

Don felt himself losing balance, then floating again. Along with the eye, he moved toward one of the side tunnels, and suddenly found himself falling down a steep slope. His stomach rolled over, as if he were riding a ferris wheel on the down side.

Abruptly the fall stopped. Don was in a dimly lit area. He was surrounded by a swirling, dense, cloud-like force. It was all over him, and all around him. It was foul and dirty, and Don struggled to breathe. He felt it trying to suffocate him. Don knew the feeling. He was facing the devil again.

The whiny voice began taunting him as before. It asked if he had given serious consideration to its former offers of wealth and power. If Don really wanted to be well, the voice said, he would go along–"because I rule the world."

All Don would have to do is say yes. All your desires will come true, the voice insists.

Don looked all around him. He could see visions of himself, restored to health. He was completely cured, and all the doctors and nurses were amazed at his miraculous recovery. His friends and business associates were showering him with gifts and attention. He was completely whole, as if nothing had happened, and completely on top of the world.

The vision made Don ache inside. He wanted it, and badly. He was tired of being pounded on the chest and stuck with horse-sized needles. He was tired of being left alone in this hospital room.

The vision continued to taunt his tired mind. Don was a celebrity. He was being touted as one who had overcome death. He was being interviewed by Johnny Carson on the Tonight show. He was rich and famous.

The voice teased him. "Do it now. Choose me, and I will give you all."

But another voice resonated deep in Don's memory: "I have chosen you. I am the Light."

Don grew suddenly angry.

"Get thee behind me, Satan!" he screamed, quoting a Scripture passage he hardly knew.

He felt as if hands were clutching him as he tried to escape the evil presence. The odor was stronger, and he felt the vomit pushing up into the back of his throat. His body felt beaten and abused. He was thoroughly terrified, yet he knew—somehow—that he was leaving.

In another dimension, Mary was at his side. Don clung to her hands desperately. He would not turn loose. He writhed and gnashed his teeth, clutching her hands as if clinging to life itself.

Hours later, when it was over, Mary's hands smelled like death. She went to a washroom and washed, but the stench would not leave. She washed again, and again, and again—but the noxious odor of death refused to go away.

It would have to wear off. It would take days.

* * *

Once again, Don began rushing through tunnels toward the white light he had seen earlier. He could sense the evil pursuing him from behind. But he heard the comforting voice of God as he flew: "You will be tempted many more times. Keep your eyes fixed on the Light, and I will guide you."

Don wished he could be back in the meadow—and he was there, resting. He knew, instinctively, that because of his persistent and foolish doubt he would go through many more trials. But he could tell, with bed-rock assurance, that God would be with him every time.

Then Don felt the familiar stirring. He was heading back to his hospital bed. He was relieved when the tunnel disappeared.

Very gently, Don felt himself slipping back into his body in the hospital room. It felt very much like scooting into a sleeping bag.

"You just kind of go in feet first," Don would write, months later, "and wiggle around until you are comfortable."

10.

Out of Body

I loved my brother.

We were in our grandfather's mulberry tree – just kids. We stuffed our faces with the sweet, juicy berries, and got our feet all stained. It was a splendid time. Like so many others, with him.

At the age of fifty-seven, Dale had a heart attack and died. I was bitter for a long time.

* * *

The nursing staff got concerned about me because I didn't want to move off my back. They gave me all the standard warnings about bedsores, and offered to give me back rubs. But I was wary. I felt, after months in the hospital, that if I moved my heart would literally shatter. My chest felt like a fragile china cabinet, with delicate glassware on all the shelves, just waiting to be smashed at the slightest touch. With every move, I could feel the china sliding around precariously on the shelves.

I felt silly, and yet I was frightened, and each feeling could only override the other for ten or twelve seconds at a time. I wanted a back rub–I ached for one–but the only way I could get one was to roll over.

Finally, after much coaxing by many nurses, I gingerly rolled over. The back rub felt great. My heart did not shatter.

Sleep would have been my most convenient pastime, except that it seemed every time I closed my eyes I'd slip from my body. Still, I couldn't hold my eyes open forever, and I eventually did get some sleep–more and more of it as the days and weeks and months dragged by.

I just could never tell when it would happen again, if ever again.

* * *

I closed my eyes, and was gone.

It was different this time. There was no tunnel. I simply rose from my body on the bed and began passing through the walls of the hospital. I could see and feel the texture of the plaster, the wood, the bricks as I passed through them, and I floated outdoors.

I saw a church. I heard organ music. It was a mournful sound. What odd music, I thought, for a church.

Into the church I floated, through the walls, and hovered above the heads of the people. Everyone looked so somber and sad. I wished they would look up and see me floating above them in my hospital gown! Maybe at least that would get a chuckle out of them! I had to stifle my own laughter, thinking about what a sight I must be. But no one noticed me.

From there I passed directly into another church, and from there into another. It was a tour of many churches, I discovered. The scene, however, and the music too, were the same in each one. Everything sad, solemn, serious.

The people's expressions seemed to indicate that they wished they were somewhere else. The few children I saw looked as unhappy as the adults.

I was no idiot. The message was clear: Our churches need joy, a sense of worship. I determined to strive for that–if I ever got out of that antiseptic prison!

I couldn't tell how long the trip was lasting. But I could feel myself slowing down. And as I passed through each new wall, into each new church, it was harder to get through the brick and stone. And I could feel myself floating lower and lower, closer to the heads of the people.

They were contemporary churches. In some of the congregations, I saw people I recognized, business associates, friends, a few relatives. I knew they were people who were not satisfied with their lives. They were there, in church, strictly for appearances' sake.

Finally, my fears came to fruition. I was stuck, halfway through a wall, unable to move in either direction. For a moment I panicked, feeling abandoned. Reason, however, took over in short order. I decided there must be some purpose in my stopping. I calmed myself and tried to think.

I considered everything I had just seen. I suddenly realized that I had been making casual judgments about these people–judgments which applied just as much to my own life! I was no different than they were!

My religious life, I knew, had been a sham. I had pursued those areas of religion that only offered temporal happiness, power, wealth, security. Mine had been a religion without sacrifice, without real commitment to the Lord–and thereby without substance.

Many times, Mary and I had gone to church, going through the motions for appearances only, wishing to be somewhere else. I knew, in that moment, entombed in the lifeless rock of a church building, that I could never hope to change others until some real and obvious changes had been made in my own thinking, my own lifestyle.

I would have to show people before I could tell them.

Having apparently learned the intended lesson, I began moving again through the wall. I breathed a full breath of fresh air, back out in the sunshine. I could see the churches receding in the distance behind me. I was glad to be gone from their musty interiors.

Then, I was back in my hospital bed, staring at the ceiling.

I was just about to ease back when I heard an alarm sound. Nurse Lynn came rushing in.

"It's not me again," I said weakly, too disappointed to make it a full-fledged question.

"Yes, I'm afraid it is, Don," she replied sadly, never breaking her pace. She began the routine of hitting my chest with her fist. Then she pushed on my chest. I could hear the anonymous Dr. Hart being summoned on the public address system. Someone was preparing the paddles. Just as they were about to apply them to me, a doctor intervened.

"He's okay now," he said, relieved. "We don't need the paddles."

I didn't even stop to think before I said what I felt.

"I've just about had it with these thumps," I said wearily. "I would really like to go home."

Before anyone could respond to me, the alarm sounded again. Again they pounded my chest, again they readied the paddles. But the thumps once again were enough. The paddles were put away.

Lynn stayed awhile to assure me I was all right. It wouldn't be long, she told me, before I would be able to go home. She even started giving me instructions for taking care of myself on the outside. I could hardly believe it. My monitor beeping–and a nurse planning for my exit date!

Lynn left, and I drifted off to sleep . . . and over the countryside. I was with Jesus Himself. I wasn't familiar with the landscape, but its beauty was breathtaking. I felt as if I didn't have a care in the world. Just being that close to Jesus somehow did it. We conversed quietly, He and I, about how beautiful and peaceful everything was. I could see clearly in all directions, with no obstructions, no pollution to mar the air.

133

I spotted a schoolyard where a group of little girls were playing. They ranged from about six to about ten years old, playing various games, singing as they played. They were enchanting to watch—until I realized suddenly that Jesus had left. But I wasn't frightened. This, after all, was the place He had brought me.

The children looked up and saw me. They watched me for what seemed like a very long time, but they acted as if this was nothing out of the ordinary. They seemed to be used to strangers floating over their heads. They continued playing their games, but they watched me at the same time.

I moved closer, and as I did I could almost feel their happiness. When I got within reach, a blonde blue-eyed little girl took my hand. I couldn't help myself; I began crying with joy. It was the first time in my life I had known such immense, brimming joy.

Unexpectedly, I was standing on firm ground. I saw my own shadow! Could this be a dream, I wondered, if I was seeing my own shadow?

<u>This is really happening</u>, I said to myself, almost with a delighted vengeance, proving to myself once again that I wasn't going crazy at all. I was overwhelmed by the reality of what was happening.

The sun was bright and warm. I could feel the little girl's soft hand holding mine. I spent a lifetime or a minute there, I couldn't say. But I played with the girls, and I listened to them sing.

And then my feet were leaving the ground, and the little girl's hand slipped away. I gently floated away from them all, and then began flying faster and faster, until I was dizzy with the forward motion. In the blur below, I thought I could make out pasture land, the colors beautiful and intense.

I was aware, then, of another presence beside me. It was Jesus.

Quietly, slowly, Jesus and I walked for the last time from the tunnel, back into the sunlight. He told me I would be leaving the hospital soon, that I had won my worst battles.

I didn't know it yet, but I had just left the darkness of the tunnel forever.

* * *

I was in my hospital bed. I felt radiant and peaceful. One of the nurses came in to check my IV.

"I am getting well," I told her confidently, "and I will be leaving very soon."

A few weeks later I was home with my family.

11.

Mary's Miracle

WITH Don in the hospital, Mary bolstered her courage by watching that crazy old television program, the one that had inspired her to quit drinking. Each time Don's condition took another of its hairpin curves, Mary called for prayer.

They finally snared her.

An older man answered the phone, listened to Mary's prayer request, and then responded, "Well, young lady, the Lord knows what your husband needs. How about you. Do you know Jesus?"

Mary froze. She had never been confronted like this. She looked down at her free hand. It held an unlighted cigarette—to her, a symbol of her aching need for something to fill the seemingly continuous void in her life. By now, under all this pressure, she was smoking up to three packs a day. And the bottom line: she knew she needed to accept Christ, personally.

The counselor gently led her to the Lord in prayer. Instantly, Mary lost her desire for tobacco. She threw away the cigarette she held and the rest of the pack as well. She never touched another one.

By the time she hung up the phone, she felt light and giddy, deliriously happy. She danced like a carefree child around the room, praising the Lord. She had finally found what she so desperately longed for, but didn't know where to find. She was unleashed. She was free.

Now–now! Everything that Don had experienced in the hospital–it all began to come clear to her. And she knew he had met Christ, too.

Mary lost no time. She had her next target already in sight. She began immediately to pray for her children.

* * *

Don came home like a newborn baby, utterly helpless. He could not go to the bathroom by himself. He could not sit or stand without help. The family drew in around him, always attentive to his needs, always ready to provide for him–and they found themselves closer together than they had ever been before.

The dream house that Don had labored so long and hard to build was now a burden. Don could certainly not keep it up, and even Mary and Jeff working together could not keep pace with the demands that such a residence required. The long, scenic driveway took hours to shovel in the snowy winters. The fantastic wood stove took logs that were taller than Mary herself! Sadly and ironically, the Brubakers sold the place—still embroiled in old legal hassles—and cleared just enough to satisfy the bank. And they found their way to a simple rented house on Belmont Street. But now, after meeting Jesus, the glamour of a dwelling place didn't mean very much at all.

As Don gained slowly in strength, his first aim was to get himself in front of a Bible. He had millions of questions, millions of ideas, from his close encounters with the spirit world. More than anything else in his life, he felt a lack of understanding, a deep longing to know. And he knew, profoundly, that God's Word held the answers. He began to spend all of his waking hours studying the Bible—literally unable to do anything else, and at first hardly able to do this for more than a few minutes at a time.

Day by day, he wrestled with the old ways of thought. He had only known sales, positive thinking, "energy forces," and the sweet allure of eastern mysticism. It hadn't clicked yet, with Don or with Mary, that groups like the group were really antichrist wolves in Christian sheepskins.

Soon Don began his personal mission: to write a book about his incredible experiences, just as God had told him to do. It was painful, tedious work. Even with a newly purchased electric typewriter, which required only the slightest touch to the keys, Don's energy sagged after ten or fifteen minutes of work. Still he sat himself down in front of the typewriter each day, determined to progress, determined to put everything on paper—to share with the world his profound encounter with eternity.

He covered the desk with notes, and then the wall in front of the desk, and then files around the desk. Each time he recalled something, each time he made some new discovery of meaning by probing the Scriptures, he scribbled it down—to find its place, later on, in his ever-growing manuscript.

And, as he probed his memory, day by day, scrounging for details, calling up those fantastic events once again in his mind, he was also engaged in the arduous process of sorting out the meaning of them all.

And slowly, beautifully, the Light began to dawn.

When Don was able to take short trips, months after his release, he and Mary naturally visited the commune. The people there, however, could smell the difference in their old comrades. The Light that Don and Mary shed automatically, as believing Christians, made the people distinctly uncomfortable.

Gradually, the commune banned the Brubakers, first by conveniently deleting them from the mailing list, then—when Mary called around to find out about upcoming events—giving them incorrect times and places. They did not want the Brubakers—who innocently but enthusiastically talked <u>all the time</u> now about Jesus—invading their turf and influencing their people.

Thus driven out of the group, Don and Mary began attending the Faith Reformed Church in Traverse City.

The kindly, soft-spoken pastor, who had visited Don often in the hospital, helped Don understand the bedrock principles of Scripture—and how human beings had distorted them through the ages. Carefully, patiently, he worked to give Don and Mary new perspectives on spirituality, on how to live for God according to His Word. Don, immersed in Scripture every day, always had dozens of questions—and got solid, biblical answers from the pastor.

Daily, Don and Mary Brubaker grew deeper in the things of the Lord. But the pastor could sense something special in Don—something very different, something weighty—that brought him to the conviction that God had tremendous ministry in store for this unusual man.

What he saw was Christ beginning to live and thrive in Don Brubaker. The same thing that bothered the other people. The same thing that bothered Don's children.

12.

The Family

BUBBLY, outgoing Cindy seemed to let everything bounce off her—nothing could bother her. But this—this bothered her. Her father, now that he was home from the hospital, could never talk about anything except Jesus Christ and praising the Lord and reading the Bible. It was obnoxious!

Whenever Cindy was around, she humored him as long as she could before changing the subject. But Dad was persistent. He would get back around to it, one way or the other. Until finally Cindy would have to find something else to do—or go crazy.

She had always been searching spiritually, even from years before, toward the end of her high school years. Inside, she was longing for answers to questions she could hardly articulate. But on the outside, she was always "just Cindy"—vivacious, happy-go-lucky, seemingly unfettered.

Drawing the strange mix of spiritual concepts she had grown up on, Cindy became a practicing vegetarian, which seemed to go nicely with a belief of reincarnation and other vestiges of eastern mysticism. When she married, Jim went along with it all, although he was never enthusiastic about it.

Reincarnation had fascinated her all along. A guy had come to the campus in Traverse City and gone into trances to tell people about their past lives, and somehow that appealed to Cindy. She could never quite work up the nerve to go up and ask to have her own past lives revealed—but she very much wanted to. The questions crowded her young mind.

But now, with Dad so determined to talk about Jesus, Cindy was distinctly uncomfortable. She didn't like hearing about Christianity—something about it made her feel odd inside.

It was the third summer after the heart attack, when Cindy was pregnant for the second time, that she finally faced the real issue that was bothering her. As her father sat down next to her on the couch and began talking about Jesus once again, Cindy suddenly exploded.

"You mean to tell me everything you told me all those years was <u>wrong</u>?"

Her father's eyes filled with tears.

"I was wrong," he said quietly.

Cindy was taken aback. It was unfathomable to her. Her father had always told her the truth. The foundations of her belief system were being shaken. It had never happened before. She didn't know how to respond.

My father was wrong.

In her confusion, Cindy simply waited. Each time the issue came to mind, she suppressed it again. But it always surfaced another time, demanding to be answered.

Over the Christmas holidays, unable to wait any longer, she finally sat down with her father at the dining room table and pointed to his Bible.

"Okay, show me" she demanded. "Show me where it says there is no reincarnation. Show me where it says it's all right to eat meat. Show me where it says everything you've been saying."

Cindy's father had been studying up for just such a moment. He opened the Scriptures and began answering every question she could think to ask.

Somewhere deep inside of Cindy, the connection was made—and the light went on.

Overwhelmed by the thorough undeniability of God's Word, Cindy began gobbling up the Scriptures herself—day after day, week after week. Sometimes she forgot to fix supper for the family because she was so caught up in the Word!

Convinced beyond all her former doubts, Cindy accepted Christ as her personal Lord and Savior. And she —like her father and mother before her—began a brand-new life.

Cindy became as irrepressible in her witness as her father was—and now she went to work on her husband. Jim was wary, but he could not deny the powerful change that he saw in his wife.

His conversion, several weeks later, was instantaneous—and beautiful.

* * *

Terrie was a reserved, bespectacled girl with a quiet artistic flair. She never spoke very loud or very fast. Hers was an observing personality.

What she observed at home disturbed her deeply. She was shocked by her father's weakened state when he left the hospital. She and Bob had come from Toronto to help, and Terrie was aghast—but privately.

She loved her father dearly. Theirs had always been a special relationship, perhaps one that can only occur between a father and his first daughter.

And now, Terrie was confused. On top of his obviously precarious physical condition, he was spouting this new "Christian" rhetoric. The group's teachings, which Terrie had held so dear, had somehow gotten lost in the mix. She was troubled, too, by the group's rejection of her parents. And, even though she and Bob had been involved with them quite heavily, she was angry at the group, and she felt like dropping out herself, out of spite.

Still, this enthusiastic born-again brand of Christianity was not her cup of spiritual tea—not at all.

At first she thought it must just be another phase, like the direct sales idea had been, years before, when she was a youngster. Or like the new religion thing, which had gone by the by. They had gotten out of that quickly enough, she remembered. Perhaps this Jesus stuff would evaporate too.

Her natural powers of observation went to work on her. Terrie watched her parents' development with curiosity. Something about them—eventually—appealed to her. After a few months, it occurred to Terrie that this had a certain quality that none of the previous philosophies had: it was genuine.

But Don and Mary were novice evangelists, and they pushed both Terrie and Bob to accept Christ. Terrie and Bob, who were both too laid-back to respond to such pressure, automatically resisted. Terrie, however, was still her father's daughter. She listened: it was her nature to listen. And she argued with him—because they had always been able to discuss an issue to its logical conclusion. Bob, ill at ease with the entire subject, generally left the room.

Don's recounting of his experiences "out of body" were not a problem for Terrie. She believed in a spirit world. She had learned well from SENA and other sources—and she knew that such things were possible. But as for Don's biblical interpretation of everything that happened—and his insistence that the place he had visited was hell—she couldn't quite piece all of that together with her belief that there was no such place, and no real evil in the world at all—and certainly no devil!

Still, Terrie realized, somewhere deep in her heart, that her parents were on to something good. And it was something that she—at least vaguely, at least momentarily—wanted for herself and her husband.

Then, suddenly, inexplicably, Don and Mary stopped

the hounding. Terrie did not know that they had suddenly realized they needed to turn the matter over to God, and let Him lead by His Holy Spirit. All she knew was that they backed off.

That was all it took for Terrie. She just needed to decide for herself. She went over to her parents' house to talk one afternoon, and she left a newborn Christian.

Don was thrilled. He was beginning to see, for the first time in his life, the true success that he had slaved for all those years.

* * *

Only Jeff was left. He would prove to be an even tougher case than his sisters had been.

He had shown none of the symptoms of typical youthful rebellion as a youngster. But his father's heart attack changed him abruptly. Left on the outskirts of town with his friends, so his mother could be close to the hospital, Jeff let his confusion and bitterness simmer. Why had his father been struck down? What purpose was there in all this chaos? What did I do to deserve this—practically losing my father?

Alcohol became a way of life for Jeff. He roamed the Traverse City party circuit. And he messed with pot.

Now, back at home, with an invalid in place of the robust father he had once known, Jeff's anger grew. He saw the change in his parents' lives, but he too thought it was another phase. He hadn't cared too much for the group, and he was skeptical of this new twist too. And as his dad talked about those weird experiences–going to hell, facing the devil, walking with Jesus –Jeff didn't know quite what to think.

Jeff often argued with his father as Terrie did, but just for the sake of arguing. He was venting his anger. He had no real intent to take any of this to heart. He only intended to keep stringing himself out, to escape, to run all the colors together and forget.

His anguish haunted him. The drinking called up suicidal urges from deep within him. One dark night, Jeff's girlfriend was barely able to stop him. He had a butcher knife poised for his stomach.

Jeff craved high speeds. Totally inebriated, he loved to push his car to the limit, around the curving streets of Traverse City in the middle of the night, with a carload of drinking buddies. Such madness had its special dangers for Jeff: he suffered from chronic night blindness, and had almost no workable vision in the dark.

Don and Mary sat at home, praying faithfully, fervently. They sensed that their son was in deep trouble. They knew no other solution.

It was the summer of 1980 when some friends invited Jeff to drive down to Orlando, Florida, for the Jesus '80 rally. Jeff didn't care much about the rally, but he thought the trip would be a great way to get a tan. His mom even paid for the trip! Who could refuse?

On the long ride south, Jeff began to conjure up second thoughts. The crowd he was with–they were straight. He realized–too late–he was going to give up the booze, the girls, and the grass on this trip. Quite a price for a lousy tan.

But the rally intrigued him. He was impressed by everyone's wide-open friendliness, even though they weren't high. And the speakers weren't too bad either. Jeff even started taking a few notes.

The Florida sun took its toll, however. Jeff sat outside the huge tent for one of the six-hour sessions, his bare back to the sun. The skin broiled and swelled, and Jeff became violently ill. All the old bitterness welled up inside him again. The trip, after all, had been a stupid move on his part.

That night, Jeff sat away from the others as they gathered on the beach around the bonfire. He was in agony with the fire on his back. The slightest movement sent sharp pain all through his body.

From his place, he could hear their singing and their talk. It made him feel heavy inside. It made him want to get away from them. He didn't recognize the convicting power of the Holy Spirit, but it was at work within him nonetheless.

He grabbed a flashlight—an aid to the night blindness—and headed toward the rest rooms, alone. He had heard his father talk to God enough to know that there was a God to talk to, so he began to complain to Him bitterly as he walked. Halfway there, unable to see clearly, Jeff stumbled and fell—and dropped the flashlight. The light went out on impact. Jeff was totally lost.

Feeling stupid, he finally made his way to the rest rooms, then returned to the group, stopping to pick up the flashlight on the way. The group was singing around the campfire; Jeff joined in.

"Well, you certainly look better," someone said to him casually.

Jeff frowned, puzzled. He blinked and turned his head away from the fire.

He could see!

The night blindness, a condition he had lived with from birth, had disappeared.

Suddenly he reached behind himself and touched his back. The sunburn had vanished. There was no pain, no sensitivity!

Tears filled his eyes, and the group gathered around him, hugging him and patting him on the newly healed back. God, so patient and loving, had pursued him to Florida, and had answered his complaining with a miracle of love.

Jeff talked to God again, and gave Him his life.

He called home long-distance and told his parents the news. Don and Mary rejoiced. Their family, finally, was one.

Christianity was a struggle for young Jeff. He had old habits to wrestle with, old friends to deal with. Alcohol and grass both had him in their grasp.

One evening, Don walked into Jeff's room and sat on the edge of the bed. He was weeping softly, like a grieving man.

"Jeff, I want you to forgive me," Don said softly, "for bringing you through these other things."

Jeff knew what his father was saying. His childhood, without the Christ-example, had been without direction.

"I forgive you, Dad," Jeff replied quietly. "And I know you and Mom are really different now. I just need more time."

Jeff's parents and his sisters stood by him in prayer, and Jeff found that God was faithful. Day by day he grew in strength, and was finally able to shed "the old man" and put on "the new."

13.

Life Goes On

THE Brubakers longed for a deeper, more expressive relationship with the Lord, and they gravitated to an independent charismatic church in Traverse City. There they flourished in the faith and, as Don's strength increased, they were given teaching and counseling responsibilities.

Don's long months and years of intensive study of the Bible gave him tremendous teaching equipment. The people of the church came to regard him as a walking concordance, able to quote Scripture from memory on virtually any topic under discussion. If he didn't have the answer to a question, he had the time to search it out.

Everything the Brubakers did now revolved around God's Word.

And the day came when they burned all their old cult books in the trash barrel out behind their rented house, renouncing their old ways of thinking. They were finally clean.

Don's love and compassion for people, his desire to see them in the Kingdom of God, became a miniature legend in the church. He became a home Bible study leader and a personal counselor to dozens. He worked with groups and individuals. As his strength grew, his calendar filled up. He found himself working the equivalent of a full-time job, just talking with people, leading them through the Scriptures to find God's answers to their needs.

He could not escape the burden God had so uniquely placed upon him. Walking through a shopping mall, he stopped suddenly and looked at the hundreds of faces swarming around him. In a moment of spiritual insight, he could see each of them as an individual, not just as part of a crowd. Each, he realized, had a different name and a unique personality. He was so overwhelmed with compassion for them that he had to bite back the tears and keep moving through the mall.

He was learning to see as Jesus saw.

Over the months and years, Don shared the story of his heart attack and his various spiritual voyages with many individuals and groups. He spoke to businessmen's groups, prayer fellowships, and churches.

And he found, as he spoke of the power of God, that people were strengthened in their faith–and miracles began to happen in their lives as well. Don and Mary saw miracles of healing and deliverance occurring all around them as they ministered to people.

There was also the ministry of prayer. Along with the elders, Don and Mary prayed and counseled with people for hours after regular Sunday services. And every week, Don's faith grew.

Still, the damaged heart was dragging him down. Years after his hospitalization, he could still barely climb a flight of stairs. A cardiac specialist saw him regularly, and Don was taking more than a dozen drugs continually. He wasn't happy about any of it.

Late in the summer of 1980, Don and Mary attended a full-gospel meeting with an evangelist whom everybody just called Brother K. Prompted by the Holy Spirit, Brother K. laid hands on Don and prayed for him—and in that moment, Don received a new heart.

From that day forward, Don walked in faith, claiming his total healing. His body was still physically weak, but Don began living in a state of victory that he had never experienced so thoroughly before.

Now as the months of victory sped by, Don determined to begin living like a man with a new heart—no longer an invalid.

Prompted to cut back on the drugs, Don determined to see a Christian doctor. Together they joined in faith and established a plan to gradually cut back on the medication.

But first, moving in the wisdom of the Spirit, Don went before the elders of his church and told them what he planned to do. Together, they agreed in prayer for a total and undeniable healing of Don's heart. Don continued claiming a thorough healing by faith, knowing beyond all doubt that he had already received a brand-new, completely healthy heart from God.

Against the odds, Don's condition steadily improved. His health increased. His strength gradually began to return. His body began revitalizing, day by day, week by week.

The doctor, ever the cautious professional, ordered a scan of the heart. Massive damage from the heart attack as well as the original genetic defect should have appeared on the report. But instead the scan showed only a general sluggishness of the heart, an appropriate condition after all it had been through–and the old war wounds of the heart attack battle itself. The genetic defect, which Don had carried from his birth, was –miraculously–gone.

God had indeed given Don Brubaker a brand-new heart–according to the measure of his faith!

And as for the "sluggishness" of the heart, Don said it was like the Apostle Paul's thorn in the flesh. Don would still have to take it easy, take life slowly. But– like Paul–nothing could keep him from rejoicing in the miracle of God's grace.

* * *

The prescribed exercise often fit nicely with Don's longing for more of God. He was ordered to take long,

Don takes Charlie for a walk.

brisk walks. On those journeys, he talked with God. Whenever he came home, Mary could tell by looking at Don's face that he had been with the Lord. His face fairly glowed. Inside, Don could sense that the healing was continuing. The search of their lives was over—now they were living in the glory of discovery.

Their lives, so jolted by heartache, were finally working.

Only one final heartache to go.

14.

One Final Heartache

I T'S a splendid February afternoon, the kind that southerners can never appreciate because they focus so exclusively on <u>temperature</u>. Michigan folk love this kind of afternoon for its clear, crisp air, its smooth blue sky, the radiant snow reflecting the sunlight.

Mary's leg ached all morning. She laid down in the bedroom with it, unable to figure out what was causing the pain. Don had picked up his Bible and come in to give her, as he often called it, "a Gos-pill." He sat and read her Scriptures and sang Scripture choruses to her, soliciting her healing before God's throne.

And, twice, he told her how very much he loved her.

Still, the aching leg has slowed her down today. It's already three o'clock now, and she isn't even dressed yet. Somehow, there's an obstruction hanging her up.

Don returns and sits down to a cup of tea in the living room, in his chair next to the wood stove. They've loved the wood stove ever since they got it; it heats the house nicely, and it's cheaper than using other kinds of fuel. And it looks so unusual, sitting there against the wall of the living room. A nifty little conversation piece.

Don is weary. Before his trip to the post office, he counseled more than the usual number of people on the phone. It seems he was on the phone all morning. And he visited a few people in their homes over the space of the past couple of days, people with deep needs, so he is weary, too, from all the activity.

They chit-chat for a few moments, then Mary gets up to head for the shower. Don stands up to add some logs to the stove.

Mary is strangely reluctant. She stops at the doorway and turns back toward him. Don looks surprised. He is standing in front of the wood stove, his hands raised slightly in front of him, as if something has startled him.

"Mary," he says simply. "Mary."

He falls backward on the floor. Mary rushes to him, turns him over, and strikes him on the chest as she has seen the nurses do in the hospital—but she does not really know how to do it, and she cannot bear to hit him more than once.

Besides, she knows—she knew from the moment he spoke—Don is gone.

It has been exactly one year, today, since Don's brother died of a heart attack.

It has been exactly five years, today, since Don suffered "clinical death" for the first time.

* * *

When Terrie calls Cindy to tell her the news, Cindy explodes with anger.

"Satan took him!" she screams at her sister.

Cindy kicks the kitchen counter, her fury boiling over. She pounds her fists and yells and cries.

Terrie patiently absorbs the outburst and, in keeping with her quiet personality, ministers peace to her sister. It takes a while, but finally Cindy settles down.

"God was never out of control," Terrie says soothingly, now that Cindy can hear her. "God is still in control. Look at the timing. It's been five years to the day."

Long after the phone call, Cindy is searching the Scriptures. It is her pattern now, after the example of her father, to immerse herself in God's Word every day.

Today—in the face of this deepest hurt—God is faithful once again to speak to His child. Hebrews 9 reaches out to touch Cindy's heart:

> For where a testament is, there must also of necessity be the death of the testator.
> For a testament is of force after men are dead: otherwise it is of no strength at all while the testator liveth.

Cindy can see it now. Her father is dead, but it is God's handiwork. Her heart begins to rejoice with gratitude.

Her father's story will be told. And it will be heard.

* * *

Saturday, Mary is preparing for the funeral. She is at peace, perhaps more so than at any time in her life. She is leaning on the Lord.

Don's doctor has told her something of a medical surprise. Don didn't die of a heart attack. His heart, thoroughly healed months earlier, simply stopped beating.

Mary, however, is not surprised. Only grateful.

She has also learned a new truth from Scripture–a truth that explains the leg ache she suffered the day of Don's death. In the Old Testament, when two people made a covenant, they sealed the covenant symbolically by placing the hand inside the upper thigh. Mary knows now that God was making a covenant with her that day–that Don's ministry would continue to live through her, through the family, through others.

She goes to her bedroom and kneels beside the bed to pray, for strength, for wisdom. Suddenly, but gently, she feels hands on her face, tilting it up. She opens her eyes and sees Don. He places his hand on her head.

"Mary, I want you to get up and do something you've never done before," he says, smiling warmly. "You'll have strength unlike you've had before. You'll continue on."

And he is gone.

Mary stands up, full of courage and determination. She intends to be a witness of Christ at Don's funeral, and afterward. She feels as if she has fallen in love with Don all over again.

And in love with Jesus.

Epilogue

THE motions of death can propel us into unlikely situations, situations that can't always be easily explained, rationally explained.

What some would call hallucinations, brought on by stress, others know to be reality—even though seemingly bizarre to the pedestrian mind.

There is more to our world than merely physical and material reality. There is the spiritual realm, existing simultaneously, yet invisibly, alongside all we see.

In this the unseen realm, the great spiritual warfare takes place. We feel the effects of the struggle, but we do not usually see the combatants. For whatever reason, some are given the exceptional eyes of faith, eyes that can look into this embattled netherworld and observe the conflict as it rages for the souls of men.

Don Brubaker was not only given this special vision, but was also given passage into the other dimension.

Escorted by the red eye of death, Don was propelled into the very midst of spiritual war. He experienced, both as observer and as participant, the incredible struggle for his own soul.

Perhaps it had to be this way, for Don. He was one who did not believe in hell, in Satan, in evil of any form. So it was that Don's soul was pulled from his pain-racked body into the very throes of hell, into face-to-face conflict with the devil. The existence of hell suddenly became all too real. Satan seemed confident: a new soul, here, to feed upon. But the battle was just beginning. God had something else in mind for Don Brubaker.

Don's experience was not only to be a confirmation of the reality of hell, however. It was also to demonstrate vividly the infinite love of a Heavenly Father, and the extreme lengths to which He will go for the sake of one of his children's souls.

In the very midst of hell, Don heard the voice of God, a voice that reassured Don that he was loved, that he was the object of a wonderful plan, that he would bear a message of love to the world from which he had so abruptly come—and that others would meet Christ because of it.

God offered Don Brubaker new hope, new life—a second chance, as it were, to meet with all the success he had longed for. Don did not waste the second chance. Having squandered forty-eight years following his own instincts, he now dug in—equipped with new, divine instincts—and became a tireless minister of the gospel.

God offers that same new hope, that same new life, to you—today. Don Brubaker's dramatic second chance is one that my never come your way. There is no guarantee of the second chance—there is only the guarantee of <u>now</u>, the guarantee that God will unconditionally forgive you of your every sin and accept you precisely as you are, when you make His Son, Jesus Christ, the Lord of your life.

Now is the time for that decision. It is almost too simple to miss—for it only requires a willingness. There are no application forms, no federal standards, no boards of review. You can approach your Heavenly Father as you are, in rags or in riches or in ruin. His love is constant—and it is searching, probing, longing for a response.

Will you respond to the Father's love?

* * *

Don Brubaker unceasingly testified of the love of his Heavenly Father. He saw relatives and friends come to Christ through his witness. He touched lives. He spread the message of Christ's gospel with sincerity, genuineness, and warmth. In his five earthly years as a Christian, Don Brubaker accomplished a lifetime of ministry.

He could not be replaced. The elders of his church eventually had to split up Don's leadership duties among two other men in the congregation.

Greg, a leader in Don's church, had perhaps the best

perspective on God's reason for taking Don home. Don, he pointed out, loved God's people, and continually petitioned the Throne of Grace on their behalf.

"Don ministered to so many," he wrote to Mary a few weeks after Don's death. "Few did not know him. Now he has become able to continue his ministry to the very feet of the Master. Our 'heavenly agent' is still doing what he loves best—giving himself to those he loved."

Mary's role, too, has expanded in the church, as she has taken up the mantle her husband once wore with such easy charm, such a loving spirit. And Jeff, after such trials in such a young life, is a genuine blessing to his family.

And so, in many ways—and in many people—Don Brubaker is still with us. And always will be.

The end.

Appendix I

Christmas 1979

Dearest Terrie and Bob,

It looks like we are going to have a white Christmas after all. We pray that the snow will hold off until we get to Cindy's however, as I do not want Mom and Jeff to have to make their first long trip in that kind of weather. It will be fun and good for all of us, this will give Jeff some much needed experience, and I think it will be good for Mom as well. And I am looking ahead for some much needed change of scenery. I think your mom and me have seen most of T.C. at least 100 times this past summer and fall. And there is just so much you can see and do here. The picture is changing however. The new mall is very nice, and we are all quite surprised at how pretty it is inside. In the middle of the mall they have a large waterfall and lots of tropical plants and foliage. The predominate trees (live) are banyan and they are about 15 to 20 feet tall. It's a good place for me to get the exercise I need. There is so much new building going on that you really won't know the place when you get back again.

I think in one of our phone conversations this fall we must have mentioned that we have looked at a lot of places for sale and a lot of them are on the water. The costs are prohibitive. It is something one might consider the taxes are too high, and if you can't find what you want, at this stage of the game we might as well rent. Or move to some place that is warm the year round. Ha ha. Seriously though we have placed this thought in the mind, we'll just have to wait and see.

My typing has improved a lot lately, however it still doesn't know how to spell or punctuate (still spells phonetically) but, the message is there? It's like the first six pages of the book. When I re-read them, I have to go over and correct almost the full page. It is coming much better though, and I know if I just kept at it I will have it done by spring. I know now what my life is to be. I just hope that we will have the courage to live up to "his" expectations. There is a lot I seem to have forgotten, especially the first six or seven days. It does come back at times, in bits and pieces and at strange times. I hope and pray that I am getting everything in the order that it should be. Everything gets a little confusing at times, and one get to feeling sort of put upon at times. Then is the time that we are truly tested. I think your Mother and me both agree on that. Ha ha. It's during these times that we have to hold each other up, change the subject or the thought and we start all over again. That reminds me of something that happened during one of my trips. That little phrase (start all over again), really has a lot of meaning. As I can remember saying or singing "We will pick ourselves up, dust ourselves off and start all over again."

We have so much to be thankful for this year, your mother and me. We have been able, the both of us, to see this beautiful growth of our children, and ourselves. I thank GOD for the wonderful experience we have all gone through. It seems to me that through so called death, we do grow spiritually, if we can but believe. We grow closer together with each passing day, even though we continue to be miles apart in reality. Terrie and Bob, do not forget any part of your experiences, not only when I went through my test, but afterward as well, don't be afraid to ask anything of our Father. Be ready to accept what you need. Just pray believing it is done and it will be. We are all still learning and growing, and we still make mistakes. But if we can just get still and listen for the answers, they are there. More and more each day I am learning that everything we really need to know is in the Bible and the more of it we read the more we can see happening in our world that makes the Bible true. Lots of people are writing lots of "stuff," but, when one is ready for the truth! it's all there in our Father's inspired word. Guess I got a little carried away there. But my dears, I believe it so much, I know where the truth is.

I think when you have the time, it would be nice for you, Cindy, Jeff and Mom to write on your reflections of this past year. I would like very much to have it printed in our Book, perhaps as reflections. Remember, this is a family project. It would not be complete otherwise. I am beginning to realize more and more what a test we all had to go through. Now that I have gone through the whole thing and come out more whole than ever, I am beginning to see GOD's rationale for this test, we must be about our Father's work at all times and when He calls we must be ready. The only way He could get my attention long enough to tell me anything was to put me where I had to listen, even though it was painful at times not only for me but for all of us. I still would not have missed this for the world.

Well my dears, I hope and pray that everything is working well for you both....We are going to miss you Sunday, but you are never far away and you are always in our thoughts. We put you both in GOD's loving care....We love you.

Mom Dad & Jeffy

Oh yes, we went to the eye doctor yesterday and he said our eyes are healthy, but we both need bi-focals. We should have them in a week or so. It was a little relief, should have known they were all right.

MERRY CHRISTMAS

Appendix II

A Reminiscence

I miss my Dad. Although he was an average man by society's standards, he was infallible to me. Even when he was so very ill in the hospital, as white as the hospital sheets, and so weak that speaking wearied him, I don't think I truly believed that death could take him....and of course, that is exactly what happened. Death did not take him, but it sure went the full ten rounds.

I don't ever remember being let down by Dad. He was always there for all of us. That is not to say he was a perfect man with no faults, what I mean to say is...whatever was going on with his own struggles in life, it was never so big or consuming that he couldn't set it aside to help his family.

I remember flying in from Toronto after the first heart attacks. We went immediately to the hospital. Dad had been through some of his hellish experiences I had yet to learn of,

and he was weak. But the first thing he said was how sorry he
was that I had to grow up so quickly. He wished I could have
enjoyed being a child longer. Fortunately, I was able to set his
heart at ease on this one count, for I never really had stopped
being a child at heart. This was mostly on account of Dad and
the way he and my mother raised us. We enjoyed so many things
as a family that allows the child inside to live. We were taught
to love, to be kind to animals, to appreciate a good practical
joke, and we always read the Sunday funnies before anything
else. We loved stories. Both my parents read bedtime stories to
us, and Dad especially would tell stories; about his childhood
or about his day...didn't matter...but what I remember is his
wonderful voice, a radio man's smooth tones, and his incredibly
contagious laughter. It's been nearly 13 years since Dad
completed his job here and left to be with the Lord...but I still
hear his voice.

I miss his advice and his ever-ready shoulder. I miss sharing
our joys and victories with him, simply because he delighted in
our happiness...and supported us in our miserable failures.

Dad was tender hearted and compassionate, almost to a
fault. The trusting nature he had landed he and my mother in
trouble more than once, but he was stubborn and fierce when it
came to his family's safety and security. That fierce love is what
finally made the greatest difference in my life. Dad had met Satan
and knew he was a beaten foe, so Dad wasn't afraid to stand

up to the jerk and command him to take his claws off the family. Believe it or not, we all resisted Dad...some of us more than others. Dad and I argued and argued about the "born-again brain washing," as I used to describe it. The more Dad tried to force me to see the error of my New Age Metaphysical ways, the harder I resisted. We were like two people pushing for all their worth on opposite sides of a swinging door. Then, suddenly, my parents quit arguing with me...simply stopped...but they began to pray. That was when I lost my balance. That was when I pushed so hard I fell...and as I fell, I called instinctively upon the One my Dad had spoken of with such conviction and absolute trust. The One who was with him throughout the terrible ordeal in the hospital and the five year journey after that. I called upon the name of Jesus, and He led me to my parents home on August 27, 1981. My mother and father took me to the bay, just down the street, and my father baptized me into the service of Christ in the waters of Grand Traverse Bay.

    Now my earthly father is gone, but there was no sting of death this time for him. Dad's body simply and quite naturally, without struggle...just dropped away. The Lord provided us with many signs and confirmations that helped us to deal with this death of the body.

    But oh, how I miss him!

Terrie Sue Brubaker Jackson
February 8, 1995

Contemplations

On January 6, 1977 everything changed. My relationship with my Mom and Dad, my relationship with my sister and brother, my relationship with my husband and my first born son, and even a relationship with a God I never knew, changed. Everything in my life changed. It changed because the one thing I could count on in this world was my father, and when he suffered his massive heart attack, my life was turned upside down, and I felt that I had been sucked through a similar dark tunnel, with no end or hope.

I loved my father dearly. In many ways, he was my best friend. He was always there to give me his wisdom. His love was never questioned, and I could always count on him. When I went to see him, lying there in the small hospital bed, after his first heart attack, it was as though my hero had turned into just a man, a man I didn't even recognize. My tower of strength was so weak that he could hardly hold his head up and talk. My best friend needed me, but I felt so helpless. All I could do was gently touch him and hold his hand. The fear of disturbing the tubes and monitors kept me from holding him and feeling his strong embrace, the embrace that would tell me this would all go away, and everything would be fine. My hero was in such pain and I couldn't do anything about it. My world was falling apart, and there was no one who could pick up the pieces.

As the days turned into weeks and the weeks turned into months, I watched my father go through a tremendous journey; a journey that took him beyond everything we had believed or even hoped for. The searching was finally over. The truth, after all of the false truths, was revealed. The old life with the old ways was gone.

When my father was sent home, the doctors literally sent him home to die. Well, God had other plans. For the next five years my father's goal in life was to tell everyone the incredible story of hell and heaven, and that most importantly included his family.

When my father died for the final time, I wanted to go with him. I didn't think I could go on without him. I just couldn't imagine not having him around. After all, God had healed him once, I thought that he would live forever. But as the Lord prompted me to read about Lazarus in the Bible, I realized that even though Jesus had healed his best friend once, Lazarus in the end also had to die a final time. The Lord was there to comfort me in my greatest time of need.

When the time had come for my father to go back through the tunnel for good, we could now let him go. We knew that we would see him again. The peace that goes beyond understanding comforted us in our time of grief. Our heavenly Father was there, comforting us.

I miss my father, even though he has been gone 13 years

now. His memory is still just as fresh as ever. As I watch my boys grow up, I see a lot of my father in them. I wish that he could see them, I wish that they could experience their grandfather's love and wisdom. I never realized how important life was until my father's life was taken away. The good news is, we will be together again. When I pass through my own life's tunnel, my father will be there to greet me, and we shall walk side by side in the presence of the Lord God Almighty.

I love you Daddy. The commission goes on.

Your Cindy Lou

Memories

The man in this book was my Dad. My recollection of the events during his illness and subsequent death were somewhat distorted at the time; by depression, alcohol and drug abuse. This time was very difficult for me and I subjected myself to these vices in an effort to avoid the pain. The illness left my father weak and frail. I was just a boy and did not want to learn to deal with life without my "strong" father.

You see, my father could do anything. He was a mountain of a man. Physically he could build or lift anything. He was a big man and I was often the envy of other kids on the block, for his mere presence portrayed safety. He was large in stature and also in intellect. Although having no formal college education, Dad could carry the floor with the best Harvard graduate and probably sell him his own house.

It was no secret that Dad wanted a boy the third time around, and when his wish was granted, he spoiled me lavishly. I can't think of much that I did not receive as a child. Dad read to me every night. He even recorded the bedtime stories so they could be played in his absence. There was even the time when he sold his high school class ring to buy me a pair of cowboy boots. There was no end to his love and understanding. Many parents say "you know you can come to me with your problems" to their kids, but few meant that statement like Dad. Dad held no judgement when I told him of a problem, he was eager to listen and always had insight.

Growing up, my parents subjected me to many different religious beliefs. The experiences written in this book, at the time, seemed like the same old story to me; Dad found a new religion. However, one thing was different. His conviction and steadfastness to this religion seemed natural. Dad really studied this new religion of his, not just on Sundays like the others before. However, I did not buy into it and went on burying myself deeper and deeper, getting farther and farther away, evermore rebellious.

One time Dad shouted, "What will it take for you to believe me? What can I do?" I responded that he could buy me a snowmobile. Dad said, "Fine. Then will you believe me?" This I know seems weird, but Dad found a way to get my attention. I figured if it was that important to him, I would listen. And for a time I was embellished in his wisdom. Dad seemed to have a glow or attraction about him. He had peace and understanding, combined with a patience I had never seen before. I even brought some of my friends by the house when they had no one to turn to, to just have Dad talk to them. No matter what time of night, Dad was always ready to console or help lost souls. (No, he did not buy me a snowmobile.)

I did not fall as deeply in love with Jesus as did the rest of my family, not right away. It took many years. Even now I do *not have a fraction of the conviction or knowledge of my Dad. I work at it daily and regret missing the opportunity that I had with my Dad to learn more, to be more like him.*

The funny thing is, I see Dad in myself more every day. Sometimes it's the way I walk or the way I can make a conversation out of nothing. Every once in a while I hear his laughter in mine, or feel his wisdom in my decisions. Often I dream about him, reliving a missed moment, but never enough.

I really miss my Dad. I look forward to the day that I can tell my own children stories until late in the night. Stories of a man bigger than life. Stories of a common man who made a difference in many peoples' lives. Stories of Don Brubaker, my Dad.

Jeff Brubaker

Jeff, Terrie, Cindy

A Memo From Mary

When I asked my three children to write a letter in retrospect I didn't realize how difficult it would be; until I, myself, sat down to write how I felt. How can you put into a few paragraphs 34 years of sharing and caring all the good times, all the trials. IMPOSSIBLE! Someday I will write a book and maybe then what is in my heart can be shared. Until then, let this book speak for itself.

There is always HOPE. Never, never give up. Your Lazarus experience or that of a loved one could be just beyond the open door and the door of love is never closed.

1st CORINTHIANS 13:4-7,13
Ref. THE BOOK

As I finish this memo my eyes go to the calendar above my desk. It is February 11, 1995!

Mary (Brubaker) Penney

Appendix III

frederick w. arnold \dds.p.c. 541 S. GARFIELD Ave.
GARFIELD CONDOFFICES

Traverse City · MI · 49684 616-941-4090

Feb 9, 1995

Dear Mary,

As Don's dentist he shared much of what he went through during his heart attack and recovery, how he struggled, and how it changed Mary's & his life.

I saw him the day before he died. He was exuberant! He said he felt as good as he'd felt in years. He all but glowed! Did he know what was to come?

In his book Don shares the experience, the hope, and faith in life that can make this part of our "Journey" much more than bearable

Fred Arnold DDS.

maranatha
family clinic

DOUGLAS J. WIGTON, D.O. ~ DOROTHY LARK, R.N., C.S.
539 E. EIGHTH ST., TRAVERSE CITY, MICHIGAN 49686   (616) 946-7360

****

Don Brubaker and I had become fairly close in the months preceding his death. His faith was uncompromising. He loved the Lord and wanted more than anything to serve Him. His first hand experience with 'life after death' made his faith all the more powerful. With this, he inspired us to the challenge of walking with the Lord along the edge.

For a time, Don's death on February 11th shattered that Christian walk. God was merciful. In His magnificent way, He demonstrated that the five years Don was given, were indeed given for us and that his leaving was part of the Divine plan. The miracles mixed in tragedy have caused us all to know that indeed in life and in death, Jesus is Lord.

****

Mary I wish you the best.

Yours in Christ,

Doug Wigton

184

❖ Appendix III ❖

DUDLEY E. BENNETT, D.O.

INTERNAL MEDICINE

DUDLEY E. BENNETT, D.O.
JOHN D. LOWNEY, D.O.
JOSEPH F. LOWNEY, D.O.
EDWARD V. REARDON, D.O.
RICHARD T. LEACH, D.O.
THOMAS J. RAIMONDO. D.O.
ANTHONY G. THOMAS, D.O.
RAYMOND J. MIS, D.O.

1050 WARWICK AVENUE
WARWICK, RHODE ISLAND 02888
(401) 467-6210

1637 MINERAL SPRING AVENUE
SUITE 302
NO. PROVIDENCE, RHODE ISLAND 02904
(401) 353-5450

5555 POST ROAD
E, GREENWICH, RHODE ISLAND 02904
(401) 884-2229

April 21, 1995

Mary (Brubaker) Penney
Peninsula Publishing
14444 Seven Hill Road
Traverse City, Michigan 49686

Dear Mrs. Penney:

Don did describe his experience as passing through a tunnel with a bright light at the end. Upon reaching the end he described the most beautiful bright lights and a feeling of being extremely relaxed and serene beyond all imagination. He described these feelings multiple times following resuscitation.

Prior to Don's description I had only read about others with similar experiences. I have always been a believer in God, creation and life after earthly death and his descriptions increased those beliefs. I would say that at the time I did not appreciate those experiences as much as I have thru the years since; having heard similar experiences from two other patients since then.

Good luck with the book and please do not hesitate to write or call if I can help further.

Sincerely,

Dudley E. Bennett, D.O.

DB/jf

Bibliography

Abanes, Richard. *Embraced by the Light and the Bible*, Horizon Books, 1994.

Eby, Richard, E. D.O. *Caught Up Into Paradise*, Baker House Co., 1978.

Rawlings, Maurice, M.D. *To Hell and Back: Beyond Death's Door*, Thomas Nelson, Inc., 1993.

Index

Red ball - eye - 77

Coming for Y   80   ⎰ Struggle f
                                       ⎱ his Soul
Temptation, mephistopheles — 84, 125
        Life review   +189 +125
                                 again, 91
Furnace, 81

Jesus, 98 & 133

"Mugwumps," doubters, 102-04

Crucifixion of X, 105-06